"Knowing when to run, walk or crawl. If you can't fly, then run, if you can't run, then walk, if you can't walk, then crawl, but whatever you do, you have to keep moving."

- Martin Luther King Jr.

The Pride of My Family

A Journey of Life Fulfilment
From Mustard Seed to a Huge Iroko Tree

Chinedum Joachim Konye Nwadike
(Rose Ann), HFSN.

Copyright © 2021 by Chinedum Joachim Konye Nwadike

All rights reserved. No part of this book may be reproduced or used in any manner without written permission of the copyright owner except for the use of quotations in a book review.

Book design by Publishing Push

ISBNs:
Paperback: 978-1-80227-026-6
eBook: 978-1-80227-027-3

Dedication

I am dedicating this book to my parents, Konye John Mmuoegbulem Nwadike and Ojukwu Agim Monica Konye Nwadike, and to our entire ancestral lineage of Konye and Nwadike families for playing unique roles in raising us. Thank you so much and may the Almighty God grant you everlasting reward and His blessings upon the living.

This book pays tribute to the other nine children of my parents: the late Dede'm Ikechi Sylvester Konye (Oganamkpa / VC-10), the late Dada'm Udaaku Clementina Konye (Mrs. Alisigwe), Dada'm Ngamaeme Jeanefrances Konye (Mrs. Dim), the late Master Onyemaechi Konye, Dada'm Anyajiwe Henrietta Konye (Mrs. Odikanwa), Dada'm Agwunihu Cordelia Konye (Mrs. Nwosu), Uloaku Ngozie Livina Konye (Mrs. Engineer Onyeajuwa), Nna'mu Onyeachisum John Bosco Konye and Ms. Chigoziri Christiana Konye. Those who are still alive, God bless you and more power to your elbows; for the dead – rest in peace.

This book is also dedicated to all the honourable grandchildren and great-grandchildren of our lineage who contributed to this noble ancestral heritage.

Recognition also goes to my uncle, the late Nna'mu Basil Anuole and the late Dada Nwaibrinta – the immediate juniors to my father, Konye – and to your entire families for your good influence on this noble family of Mama Ogoma Nwadike.

The final dedication is to my paternal motherland, my maternal motherland, and my in-laws for facilitating this work of extending our linage. To God be the glory.

Dedication

I am dedicating this book to my parents, Konye John Mmuoegbulem Nwadike and Ojukwu Agim Monica Konye Nwadike, and to our entire ancestral lineage of Konye and Nwadike families for playing unique roles in raising us. Thank you so much and may the Almighty God grant you everlasting reward and His blessings upon the living.

This book pays tribute to the other nine children of my parents: the late Dede'm Ikechi Sylvester Konye (Oganamkpa / VC-10), the late Dada'm Udaaku Clementina Konye (Mrs. Alisigwe), Dada'm Ngamaeme Jeanefrances Konye (Mrs. Dim), the late Master Onyemaechi Konye, Dada'm Anyajiwe Henrietta Konye (Mrs. Odikanwa), Dada'm Agwunihu Cordelia Konye (Mrs. Nwosu), Uloaku Ngozie Livina Konye (Mrs. Engineer Onyeajuwa), Nna'mu Onyeachisum John Bosco Konye and Ms. Chigoziri Christiana Konye. Those who are still alive, God bless you and more power to your elbows; for the dead – rest in peace.

This book is also dedicated to all the honourable grandchildren and great-grandchildren of our lineage who contributed to this noble ancestral heritage.

Recognition also goes to my uncle, the late Nna'mu Basil Anuole and the late Dada Nwaibrinta – the immediate juniors to my father, Konye – and to your entire families for your good influence on this noble family of Mama Ogoma Nwadike.

The final dedication is to my paternal motherland, my maternal motherland, and my in-laws for facilitating this work of extending our linage. To God be the glory.

About the Author

The author is Chinedum Joachim Konye Nwadike, HFSN. She is an indigenous daughter of Orlu Town in the Orlu Local Government Area of Imo State in Igboland of South-eastern Nigeria. A naturalised citizen of the USA, she earned her PhD from Lacrosse University LA, USA. She is a  missionary in London, saving lives at different abortion clinics and helping vulnerable young mothers with pregnancy crises. She is also a Child Care Practitioner. Sister Chinedum was the first Zonal Superior of The Holy Family Sisters of the Needy, English Zone, United Kingdom. She is currently the promoter and coordinator of the Holy Family Sisters of the Needy Missionary Appeal in the U.K. She is the author of *Building Up Self-Confidence A Fundamental Way of Conquering Fear.*

She can be contacted at
chinedumnwadike@yahoo.com

Acknowledgements

My heartfelt gratitude goes to Chief Nze Bernard NI Onunaku, my former USA academic classmate, for taking the time to moderate this project. Chief, thanks so much.

Aunt-Dada'm Lady Theresa (nee Agim) Agu, thanks immensely for writing the foreword. May God continue to shower His blessings upon you and your family.

The late Dede'm Mr. Ikechi Sylvester Konye, Adanne'm Jane Dim, Dada'm Henrietta Odikanwa, Dada'm Cordelia Nwosu, Ogom Engineer Declan Onyeajuwa, Nwanne'm Mr. Simon Chukwuemeka Nwadike, Nwanne'm Mrs. Livina Engineer Onyeajuwa, Nna'mu Mr. John Bosco Konye, Nwankenta Christiana Konye and Aunt Lady Theresa provided information that enriched this write-up. May the Almighty God provide for you in time of need. I am very grateful for your help.

I owe enormous thanks to Rev. Brother Joachim Ezetulugo of the Marist Brothers of the Schools for taking on the responsibility of editing this work. Brother, thanks a lot, and God bless you.

About the Author

The author is Chinedum Joachim Konye Nwadike, HFSN. She is an indigenous daughter of Orlu Town in the Orlu Local Government Area of Imo State in Igboland of Southeastern Nigeria. A naturalised citizen of the USA, she earned her PhD from Lacrosse University LA, USA. She is a missionary in London, saving lives at different abortion clinics and helping vulnerable young mothers with pregnancy crises. She is also a Child Care Practitioner. Sister Chinedum was the first Zonal Superior of The Holy Family Sisters of the Needy, English Zone, United Kingdom. She is currently the promoter and coordinator of the Holy Family Sisters of the Needy Missionary Appeal in the U.K. She is the author of *Building Up Self-Confidence A Fundamental Way of Conquering Fear.*

She can be contacted at
chinedumnwadike@yahoo.com

Acknowledgements

My heartfelt gratitude goes to Chief Nze Bernard NI Onunaku, my former USA academic classmate, for taking the time to moderate this project. Chief, thanks so much.

Aunt-Dada'm Lady Theresa (nee Agim) Agu, thanks immensely for writing the foreword. May God continue to shower His blessings upon you and your family.

The late Dede'm Mr. Ikechi Sylvester Konye, Adanne'm Jane Dim, Dada'm Henrietta Odikanwa, Dada'm Cordelia Nwosu, Ogom Engineer Declan Onyeajuwa, Nwanne'm Mr. Simon Chukwuemeka Nwadike, Nwanne'm Mrs. Livina Engineer Onyeajuwa, Nna'mu Mr. John Bosco Konye, Nwankenta Christiana Konye and Aunt Lady Theresa provided information that enriched this write-up. May the Almighty God provide for you in time of need. I am very grateful for your help.

I owe enormous thanks to Rev. Brother Joachim Ezetulugo of the Marist Brothers of the Schools for taking on the responsibility of editing this work. Brother, thanks a lot, and God bless you.

I lack words to express my gratitude to Ogom Engineer Onyeajuwa Declan and his wife, Mrs. Livina Onyeajuwa, for their contributions to the success of this production. May God reward you abundantly.

Thanks, Dede'm Enyinneya Nwadike, for being such a good representative of our family in the USA. God bless you and your entire family.

My profound appreciation goes to my nephew, Mr. Kelechi Camillus Odikanwa, all my nephews and nieces, and my cousin, Mr. Chinedu H. Agu. I really appreciate your involvement.

Chinedum Joachim Konye Nwadike, HFSN.

Foreword

I am delighted that Reverend Sister Dr. Chinedum Konye Nwadike gave me the privilege of writing the foreword to this inspirational book.

This book, in a nutshell, is an account of ancient Igboland wise family planning. As we follow the trail and trend of the narration, we can see, touch, feel and experience the very exciting fabric of the Konyes' lives. In Igboland in Southeastern Nigeria, and in Africa in general, since slavery depopulated the original people, it became customary for African men to take many wives in order to raise many children as it was not always possible to get many children from one woman.

But Konyezuruyahu John Nwadike, adept in family planning and blessed with a woman with high-fecundity, high-fidelity, and high proliferation, was able to raise ten children, all two years apart. Interestingly, Konye dedicated his daily occupational proceeds to raising and educating all the children. His entire life was spent in the procurement of materials, food, and finances to ensure the good upbringing of his children.

As a result, he was both envied and deprived, but with his Chi-God behind him, he prospered. He realized that the prestige and power of parents are enhanced when the children are well-groomed, well-bred, and well-educated. We say: *Nwabuike, Nwabugwu, Ikesinanwa or Odikanwa – onweghi ihe dikanwa.*

Much more tactical was the legacy of hard work, dedication, persistent pursuit of an ideal and the resulting success and clean-breasted expenditure of personal energy deriving from internal resources, all willed to the present generation and future generations.

Although he did not live long enough to see the glory of his labour expressed in the way his children have been correspondingly blessed with numerous children, good education, and prosperity, his is a model family worthy of emulation. He was not devastatingly rich; nevertheless, his strong will to perform illuminated his path to success. As we say in Igboland, *Iga echi na obi Nwata, rie na obi ogaranyi.* Coincidentally, an English authority reiterates, "How blest is he who crowns in shades like these, a youth of labour with an age of ease." Goldsmith - Famous Quotes, Webster Encyclopaedia of Dictionaries compiled by John Gage Allee, PhD (p. 837).

Konyezuruyahu John and Ojukwu Monica Agim Konye Nwadike laboured in their youth so that their children, grandchildren and great-grandchildren might have "an age of ease" – *rie no obi ogaranyi*. Let us proceed now with zesty haste to read what has been laid out in front of us.

Aunt Lady Theresa Agu (nee Agim)

Contents

Dedication   v

About the Author   vii

Acknowledgements   viii

Foreword   x

Preface   xv

Introduction   1

Chapter One   The Origin of My Family (Konye)   5

Chapter Two   The Beginning of the Konyezuruyahu   13

Chapter Three   A Gallery of Functions of the Family   145

Chapter Four   The Prestigious Accomplishments of the Family   147

Chapter Five   Photographs from the Family Album   155

Chapter Six   My Father's Brothers and Sisters   199

Chapter Seven	A Guiding Light to Future Generations	201
Summary		203
Conclusion		213
About the Author		215
Bibliography		219

Preface

On that day, the plant that the Lord has grown shall become glorious in its beauty, and the fruit of the land shall be the pride and splendour of the survivors of Israel. Then those who are left in Zion, who remain in Jerusalem, every one enrolled in the book of life, shall be called holy. (Isaiah 4:2-3)
- The Jerusalem Bible,
Popular Edition 1974 (p. 976)

The above quotation coincided with my aspiration to write this book. My parents began their lives without us till God Almighty sowed the seeds in them and they produced ten of us. The nine surviving children grew up in beauty, wisdom and integrity, and our own seeds spread across the globe. Those who are still young, who have been left behind by our parents and elders, are still striving to make it, as our ancestors did. Those of us who are able to make it successfully, as our parents and elders did, will be the pride of the Konye family, and they shall be called the legitimate children of our lineage.

The Konyezuruyahu Mmuoegbulem family is like the Iroko tree that begins as a tiny seedling and grows to a gigantic height, spreading its branches far and wide. The Iroko tree is a symbol of anything that starts tiny and expands to a great size. This is how my family began – with one man – and increased to many families with different talents. We have farmers, traders, a typist, computer engineers, consultants, teachers, an electrician, nurses, a doctor, accountants, a reverend sister, a reverend father, students, etc.

Members of our family are experts in different walks of life. It wasn't like that in the beginning when our father started with our mother. In our noble family, Papa was a farmer, wine-tapper, sawyer and trader. Mama was a farmer, as well, and a market woman. Dede'm Ikechi Sylvester (Oganamkpa / VC-10) was a successful retired secondary school teacher, while Dada'm Clementina was also a successful market woman. Onyemaechi was just a teenager when he passed on, but he was known as a prophet. Dada'm Jeanefrances is a full-time housewife, Dada'm Henrietta is a progressive trader and Cordelia is another successful retired teacher. Nkechinyerem Rose Ann, now Chinedum, is a Reverend Sister, Doctor of Philosophy Psychology, and also used to be a registered Christian counsellor in the United Kingdom. Livina, a successful retired teacher, is now a business tycoon. John Bosco, once a well-known businessman in Jos Plateau State, is now a business manager in Orlu Main Market, and Chigoziri is a progressive businesswoman. Among our grandchildren we have Rev. Fr. Leonard as a high priest of God, Desmond a business manager, Ferdinand an accountant, Okuckwuch with a diploma in Law, Camillus a well-known business manager in Lagos, Juliet a nurse in Spain, Ijeoma Alagwu a nurse in the USA, Ugochukwu a French teacher, Chidara doing computer engineering, Chigozie Vincent Konye an electrician, Viviana studying Education Biology at Imo University and Chinaemerem nursing in Nigeria. If I enumerated them all, this book would be much longer.

I came across a book titled *Pride of Black British Women* by Deborah King that motivated me to write this book on the Konye family. I immediately started assembling material. As the English adage says, every disappointment is a blessing. That was exactly what happened in my case. I was able to write this book because I was on a sickbed. I'd had surgery on my big toe for a bunion and was walking with two crutches. I had to stay home for six weeks. My mind flashed back to the book I'd read three years ago, and I started writing without hesitation. I called Beckton Globe Library, East Ham, to ask whether they had the book. They did not but were able to reserve it from Willesden Green Library, the original place I'd borrowed it from. Amazingly, it was exactly the same copy. The sign I'd made on a spot while I was reading it served as the identification mark. God is great! Opportunity comes but once. As I started to write, ideas flowed like a river. With God all things are possible!

My objective in writing is to pass on to the younger generations the knowledge of how we began, about who our father and mother were, the type of life they lived, the legacy they left behind. The efforts they made to raise us. Also, to reveal the kind of parents our own parents had, that is, our paternal and maternal grandparents.

Papa and Mama lived good lives, they loved their neighbours and they were generous and kind-hearted. They disliked and shunned injustice, though they were victims of injustice. They never compromised on speaking the truth, no matter the effect on them. We, the next generation, are still suffering from the maltreatment some people meted out on us for being truthful. However, we don't mind, and we must keep on pressing on as they did.

Despite their low income and their low-class status, they were able to educate us to the highest academic level. They worked hard to feed themselves and maintain their family. Their children never suffered **kwashiorkor** during the Nigerian-Biafran Civil War that broke out in 1967 and ended in 1970. They were uneducated according to conventional education, but they were wise and naturally intelligent. Papa and Mama used to speak to us in proverbs and sign language. Most of the time, they used their eyes, shaking their heads and shaping their mouths to talk to us. Initially, they were non-Christians but were later converted to Catholicism and died as baptised Christians.

The main purpose of writing this is to let you, the younger generation, know that Papa Konye John and Mam Ojukwu Monica were not dubious individuals or lazy fellows. They lived good lives and imparted to their children the right way of living. They were great achievers, and we, their offspring, must continue their great work. We need to celebrate their greatness and success because they made us proud.

As we do this, let us not lose sight of the Creator who inspired our parents and still infuses His blessings to enable us to emulate them. Without God we can do nothing. I commend you to keep on lifting up the legacy they left for us. Never allow it to vanish from your sight. Keep on burning the everlasting candle of our family integrity and glory. Do not be afraid. Remember that there must be obstacles on the way, but keep moving on. Obstacles and fear do exist but will not prevent you from succeeding. When you succeed, it means you are shaking off your obstacles and fears and embracing victory. Victory is yours. As a result, you will help maintain our family self-confidence. Martian Luther King Jr., the famous leader of the Civil Rights Movement in the USA, wrote in one of his research projects, "Keeping moving forward: knowing when to run, walk or crawl. If you can't fly, then run, if you can't run, then walk, if you can't walk, then crawl, but whatever you do, you have to keep moving forward." I advise you, my people, to keep moving on, doing anything that is creditable to earn a living. If you can't be a medical doctor, then be a nurse, if you can't be a nurse, strive to be a counsellor, if you can't be a counsellor, then be a teacher, if you can't be a teacher, then be a trader, if you can't be a trader, be a farmer, or accountant, or hairdresser, or typist, or electrician, or footballer, etc. The most important thing is that you are doing honest work to earn a living and enhance someone's life. All fingers are not equal; do what you can to succeed in life. Our parents made a huge success by doing menial jobs. One should know that it is not only in academics that one can claim success and victory but in any effort one makes to make life worth living. Once you are able to take on responsibilities, executing daily decisions and tasks, motiving and directing someone else to succeed in his or her career, you have something to be proud of. Therefore, be proud of your achievements and keep on motivating each other. Counsel, advise and instruct each other because it is not only gifts of money, food or clothing that help a person; your good advice could help someone to become a king. Dede'm Ikechi became an effective teacher because he heeded Aunt Theresa Mrs. Agu's advice. I became a Reverend Sister because I listened to Mama's guidance and followed in the spiritual footsteps of the Marist Brothers of the Schools. Most of us succeeded because we paid attention to the instruction of our parents and elders. A word is enough for the wise. If you are able to work and feed your children, train them, and uplift someone else, it will give you satisfaction; and if you're able to make right judgements, you are a great achiever. So, be content with your good efforts. Be proud of the Konye family; be delighted with her heritage and legacy. And may we live in a manner worthy of our parents and ancestors. Let us continue being witnesses of the noble legacy they left us. The facts you will appreciate as you read along are enumerated below:

1. Genealogy of the Konye family
2. Who started the family?
3. How did the family grow from one man and one woman to many people?
4. How the family advanced and succeeded

Rev. Sr. Dr. Chinedum Joachim Konye Nwadike, HFSN
(Nkechinyerem Rose Ann Konye Nwadike)
12th November 2014

Introduction

I am writing this book to x-ray the ancestral origin, the advancement, and the greatness of our parents and us, their offspring. This book is titled *The Pride of my Family* and will highlight, in detail, all the things that led to "the fulfilment" of our noble family.

As I wrote in my book *Ancestral Legacy of Family Counselling*, parents play a vital role in the lives of their children. Our first counsellors, teachers, and leaders in our lives are our parents and relatives. However, in this present era, peer groups, television, the internet, and Facebook are taking the upper hand in the upbringing of children and everyone is feeling the unhealthy consequences. Basic home training is crucial in the life of every child. This training is ultimately going to be reflected in the pride of the Konye family, from our ancestors to our present generation. Our parents, relatives and elders are the first role models we encounter in our lives. Why do we need role models in our lives? We need role models because they enhance the healthy development of our families, our villages, towns, society, and the world at large. Role models produce positive images that both adults and youth are motivated to embrace. Our parents inspired us to be hardworking children and lovers of education, even though they weren't formally educated. Nevertheless, their role modelling enabled us to strive towards the attainment of successful academic careers. *The Pride of my Family* focuses on all the aspects of career advancement, such as educational and career achievements and the successes of the entire Konye family. Today, we have professionals in all walks of life.

What Is "Pride" In This Context?
"Pride" in this context means the prestige of the family. What makes the family honourable, what role did adults play in the life of the children, what is the family known for? What legacy did our ancestors pass on to us? For instance, their good name, good acts, generosity, culture, wisdom, sound administration and religion that make the family prestigious. Is the present generation advocating this noble legacy? These questions will be answered and explained in the body of this book.

What is Family?
Family, in the African context, means the group of people who are related by blood and come from one common ancestor. What the English refer to as nephews and nieces, cousins and aunts, are regarded in Africa as brothers and sisters; this is family in our context.

Family is like an Iroko tree that begins as a seedling and grows into a well-developed plant that blossoms yearly to produce good fruit or bad fruit. In my own family, my father and mother are the huge trees that together produced ten fruitful trees that spread across the village and beyond.

In every family, parents are the primary caretakers, nurses, teachers, counsellors, directors, theologians, psychologists, psychotherapists and leaders. The elders and relatives are secondary caretakers. Our parents play vital roles in the lives of their children. Each child is a typical carbon copy of either the father or the mother; sometimes a child alters this makeup by acquiring new behaviour from a peer group, which often has devastating results. Our parents influenced us a lot, and this manifests in the way each of us uniquely behaves, talks, reasons, acts, walks, looks, eats and dresses. What we are is what we learnt from our parents and relatives, as well as the influence of the company we keep. We were privileged to obtain full basic home training from our parents. Our parents and ancestors left a remarkable legacy for us to imitate. I will enumerate in this book those things that contributed to the greatness and pride of our noble family.

What are the New Members doing to Raise the Prestige of the Family?

The new members of the family, who are of our generation, are making immense efforts to build on the good foundation laid by our parents. Many are married and have many children. Some, including nephews, nieces and cousins, are farmers, businessmen and women, educators, counsellors, nurses, psychologists, accountants, electricians, engineers, soldiers, etc.

Why Does Family Prestige Matter?

Each family is proud of its name because of the reputation attached to it. Our father was a very determined person; what he decided to do, he would carry out. He was a great achiever and always sustained his efforts till his goal was accomplished. He was an honest, truthful and peaceful man. He relied on his God for his lifestyle. He was faithful to his wife. Papa was generous and kind. In his youth, his neighbours took away his land, but he did not give up and succeeded in reclaiming his lands and palm trees. He was very successful with one wife and had many children. He knew the importance of education so ensured that his children obtained a high-quality education.

Chapter One
The Origin of My Family (Konye)

Every family originated somewhere, as the Konyezuruyahu (Konye) family did. In this book, readers will learn how the Konye-Nwadike family came into existence – the kind of lives our ancestors and my parents lived, their occupation, religion, food, and their advancement till the present time through their offspring. At this juncture, I am going to narrate, in a nutshell, the ***ancestral origin of* Nwadike,** the biological father of my own blood father, Konyezuruyahu Mmuoegbulem Nwadike.

Our Family began with Amuba

The name Amuba means "increase in number". In the book of Genesis (1:28), God created man and woman and said, "Be fruitful, multiply, fill the earth and conquer it." Our family took this seriously and is increasing to infinity non-stop! According to the narrative of the late Ikejiofor Sylvester

Konye (Oganamkpa / VC10), our family originated from Amuba, who was the father of Nwadike. Then Nwadike married two wives, **Mama Ogoma and Nne Alaekwe**, who were from the same father but not from the same mother. Dike and Abiriba were from the same father (Ekewaloe) and same mother. Dike gave birth to Ogoma, while Abiriba gave birth to Alaekwe. Both women were from Umudara Umuna, from the family of Dike and Abiriba Ekewaloe. Ogoma and Alaekwe married the same man – Nwadike, our grandfather. Mama Ogoma gave birth to our father, Konyezuruyahu, Anuole Basil and their sister, Nwaibirinta. Our father's maternal land is Umudara Umuna. Alaekwe gave birth to our father's half-brothers, Mgaja, Raphael and Geoffrey, and some girls. Konyezuruyahu was born in a polygamous and non-Christian family. Konyezuruyahu Mmuoegbulem married Ojukwu (from Umuokwaraibewe), Umokwarairobe-Umusasa and Uzo-ubi **Odududike**. **Agim**, the son of **Osuduroka**, married Ojiobianu Nneyidiya of the Umuobu Umuowa family in Onyeka and family in Umuojinma-Umuowa.

Agim and Ojiobianu had five children: Titus, Adaeriri, Ojukwu (our mother), Augustine and Theresa.

Now, our family line went from Amuba to Nwadike to Konye and spanned four generations. In Igboland in Eastern Nigeria, each name given to a child has significance and relates to circumstances surrounding the child's birth.

And it always manifests according to their wishes. The main fact here is that we, the children of Konyezuruyahu and Ojukwu, are from good family backgrounds, and most importantly, we are from the ancestral lineage of Nwadike and Konye of Ndiowerri village in Orlu, Imo State, in Eastern Nigeria. As a result of our good family background, our uncle, Chief Mgaja (our father's half-brother) and our father, Konye, married into the same family of Agim, our maternal home. Our mother, Ojukwu, and Dada Adaeriri were children of the same father and mother – Agim and Ojiobianu.

So, uncle Chief Mgaja married Adaeriri, who was the immediate elder sister of our mother, and Konye, our father, married our mother, the immediate younger sister of Adaeriri. Dada Adaeriri and Mama Ojukwu married into the same family of Nwadike. It happened this way because of their good family background and their good relationships and behaviour. Our uncle, chief Mgaja, after his marriage to Dada Adaeriri, renamed her Oyiridiya, meaning a woman who resembles her husband. Then Dada Adaeriri became popularly known as Oyiridiya. Papa Konye retained our mother's original name, Ojukwu, but added to it Ojukwu-nwereugo, meaning honourable beautiful lady.

Dada, Adaeriri and Mama Ojukwu were role models of their era and our own time, respectively. They were the pride of our families and women to be emulated.

Konye Family Tree 1913 - 1980

Nwadike had two wives – Ogoma and Alaekwe. Nwadike and Ogoma begot Konyezuruyahu, Anuole Basil and Nwabirinta. Nwadike and Alaekwe begot Mgaja, Raphael, Geoffrey and some girls. Konyezuruyahu was born in 1913 and married Ojukwu, with whom he begot ten children, who, in turn, begot forty-two children.

1. Ikechi Sylvester and his wife Chika Comfort begot five children.
2. Udaaku and her husband, Alisigwe Felix, had no children.
3. Onyemachi passed on when he was a teen.
4. Ngamaeme Jeanefrances and her husband, Dim Osuala, begot ten children.
5. Anyajiwe Henrietta and her husband, Onyemauchukwu Odikanwa, begot seven children.
6. Agwunihu Cordelia and her husband, Oguadimma Nwosu, begot five children.
7. Nkechinyere'm Rose Ann became Reverend Sister Chinedum Konye Nwadike, PhD.
8. Uloaku Ngozi Livina and her husband, Azuanuiwe Onyeajuwa, begot five children.
9. Onyeachusim John Bosco and his wife, Chinyere Anthony, begot five children.
10. Chigoziri is a self-sufficient spinster.

Konyezuruyahu Nwadike Family Tree 1913 - 1980

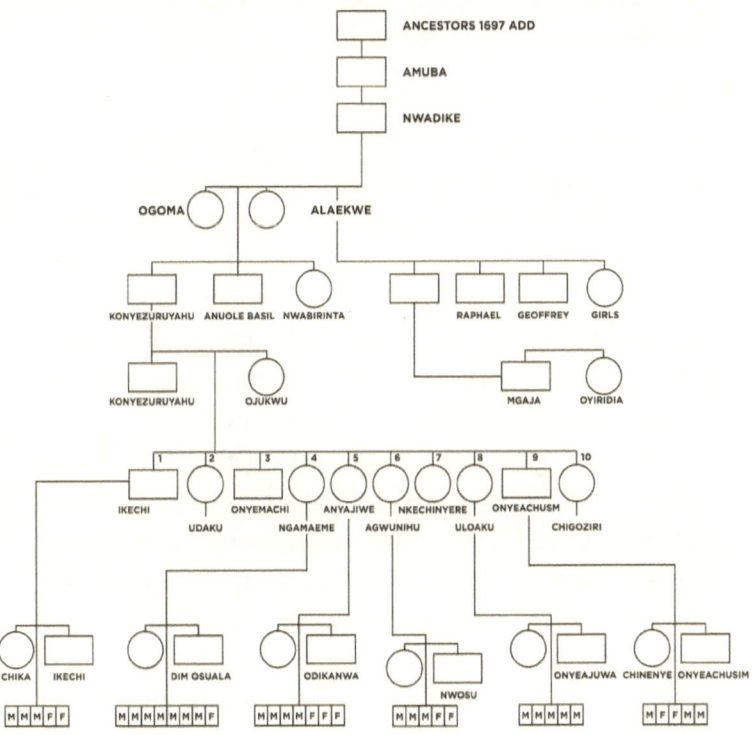

Who Started the Family?

How did the Family Grow from One Man and One Woman to many People?

In Psalm 89, God made a promise to His servant, David, that his dynasty would last forever. Amuba, our ancestor, also inherited this pledge from God because we are descendants of David and Abraham; we keep on multiplying like the sand of the seashore and our descendants increase forever. If we take 54 years as the average lifespan of a generation, we should go back about 216 years to the beginning of the family – that is, 1697 AD, counting back from 1913 AD. Our family has grown very large, and procreation is an ongoing cycle.

When we gather for a family get-together, the house is full of people bustling around, just like bees in a beehive. We are great children; we are blessed children, and we are happy children of Amuba. Even though we are surrounded by ups and downs (which are part of nature), we will continue progressing. As I write along, I will mention the names of personalities in all walks of life to support my position. At this stage, I am going to tell you about the origin of Nwadike, our ancestor, the biological father of Papa Konyezuruyahu Mmuoegbulem – how it all began, in a nutshell. In Igboland, each name given to a child at birth relates to the circumstances surrounding the child's birth. The name of Nwadike, our father's father, means "son is strong." His parents gave him the name because they perceived him as a person who would be brave and powerful, and their assumption materialized. Nwadike grew up with strength, married many wives and begot many children. Moreover, as a powerful man, he secured many lands for farming.

Amuba was the father of Nwadike, and Nwadike was the father of our father, Konye. **Amuba's** name means "**increase and multiply**", and if I start narrating the descendants of Amuba down to our present generation, you will observe that we are more than a country. But I am going to narrow down my account to Nwadike and the details of the family of Konye, our legitimate father. My elder brother, the late Ikechi Sylvester Konye, explained our ancestral origins thus:

> *"We are born in the family of Konye Nwadike.*
> *Konye was born in a polygamous family; his junior*
> *brother is Mr. Aniole Nwadike.*
> *Their other brothers were Mr. Mgbaja Nwadike,*
> *Raphael and Geoffrey.*
> *Nwadike was the son of Amuba.*
> *Amuba was a son of Okwaraojiaku.*
> *Okwaraojiaku was a son of Okwaranosike.*
> *Okwaranosike was a son of Okwaraofor.*
> *Okwaraofor is our present Ndiowerre village."*

Written by my elder brother, the late Ikechi Sylvester Konye, in the year 2010.

This is our ultimate pride; we are increasing and multiplying, as well as growing from strength to strength.

Chapter Two

The Beginning of the Konyezuruyahu

Mmuoegbulem Family History

1. Family Personalities and Expansion
2. Social Functions and Occupations
3. Educational Attainments
4. Religious Achievements
5. Community Activity Participation

One should ask, who was Konyezuruyahu Nwadike? Konye was the first son of Nwadike from his mother's side, Ogoma Nwadike. As stated in Chapter One, he has two blood siblings from his mother's side, namely, Anuole Basil and Nwaibirinta. Our father, Konye, was born in 1913 in a polygamous family. He was given two names by his parents at birth (Konyezuruyahu and Mmuoegbulem). Konyezuruyahu means "what I have is enough for me" or "I am contented with what I have", while Mmuoegbulem means "let me not be affected by the anger of gods." We, his children, nicknamed him Diokpa, meaning an experienced old man.

Our parents enjoyed a happy marriage and lived happy lives with their children. They had ten of us, and they gave us both basic home training and academic education. You will see the effect of this as you read along. You will be an eye witness of the fruitfulness of this upbringing in the lives of their offspring through their advancement in life.

The pride of the average Igboland man of Eastern Nigeria is in the number of children he has and has raised. Below are the ten crowns (children) of Papa Konye and Mama Ojukwu Konye Nwadike:

Our Original Names

1. Ofojiogu Ikejiofor Sylvester
2. Odaaku Clementina
3. Onyemachi Prophet
4. Ngamaeme Jeanefrances
5. Anyajiwe Henrietta
6. Agwunihu Cordelia
7. Nkechinyerem (Ngbeke) Rose Ann
8. Uloaku Livina
9. Onyeachusim JohnBosco
10. Chigoziri Christiana

In Igboland, a man with many children is also counted among those who are wealthy. Accordingly, Papa was one of the wealthy men.

A Tribute in Honour of Papa and Mama as it is Biblically Written in the Book of Ecclesiasticus

> *"Next let us praise illustrious men, our ancestors in their successive generation. Here is a list of generous men whose good works have not been forgotten. In their descendants, there remains a rich inheritance born on them. Their descendants stand by the covenants and give thanks to them, so do their children's children. Their offspring will last forever, their bodies have been buried in peace, and their names live on for all generations. The peoples will proclaim their wisdom; the assembly will celebrate their praises."*

Ecclesiasticus 44:1, 10-15
The Jerusalem Bible, Popular Edition
Darton, Longman & Todd 1974, (p. 957).

Today, I am writing in remembrance of our parents who made an arduous effort to bring us up and make us what we are today. Despite all the ordeals they went through, they succeeded in life and in nurturing us. In our time, we are facing the same ordeal. Therefore, let not give up hope but keep marching forward to make more of a success than they did, bearing in mind the inspiration of the famous USA Civil Rights Activist, Martin Luther King Jr., who urges us thus:

> ***"Knowing when to run, walk or crawl. If you can't fly, then run, if you can't run, then walk, if you can't walk, then crawl, but whatever you do, you must keep moving forward."***
>
> *Source: https://www.goodreads. comquotes26963-if-you-can't-t-fly-then-run-if...*

Therefore, be courageous, and keep striving till you succeed. Without suffering one cannot pave one's way. Remember, what you believe can lead you through or set you back.

The Lifestyle of Papa Konye Nwadike

Papa Konyezuruyahu was a handsome man, fair in complexion and about six feet tall, with long arms and legs. He was slim and fit, with a small skull and an oval face. He was peaceful and gentle in outlook and in deeds. He was very humble and generous. He was a God-fearing man, honest and sincere, and always frowned at injustice. He was a man of his words; his yes was yes, and his no was no. Papa never gave way or stepped down for injustices, no matter how threatening the situation. Papa was fearless and brave, a man of integrity and standing. He was not afraid to suffer for standing for truth and justice; he never feared any ills or evils and always trusted his Chi (God) to lead him. I often heard him saying, "My Chi will lead me." This Chi leading him made me choose the name **Chinedum** (meaning God leads me) during my religious profession initiation. Our mother's utterances, as well, made me choose the name Chinedum. Papa never bothered anybody, but if troubled by anybody, he would defend himself to the hilt in a nonviolent manner, like the American Martin Luther King Jr. and Mahatma Gandhi of India. Papa believed in "live and let live," and if anyone did not want him to live, he would placatingly ask why. Papa always used to put this proverb across: *amutara ogbe nwa ka o kpagbuo ibe ya*. It means "one who is an elephant should not behave like one" or "a fat child is not born to squeeze the tiny ones."

As an honest man, he maintained a peaceful attitude and had an open-door policy. He practised justice, truthfulness, sincerity and generosity and had a great capacity for forgiveness. For those of us in Igboland, it is part of our lifestyle to quarrel and squabble, but whenever it happens, we always forgive and get along. When neighbours had a dispute, the entire community would gather together to settle the matter. At that time, our elders used to speak the truth. It was a time when our elders used to call a spade a spade, black- black, and white- white. It was also a time when our elders took no bribe from anybody and were ready to bear any consequences of speaking the truth.

At that time, whenever families had a disagreement, they settled it amicably and moved on. No one would think of harming the other, and if anyone dared to do so, our ancestors would deal with the person. It was a time when brothers and sisters loved and cherished one another with their whole hearts and with due respect. It was an era when there was less jealousy and when everybody rejoiced in what others had achieved. This changed a lot in his life time but never compromised his dignity; rather, he worked harder to thrive, despite his lack of academic skills. Therefore, I advise you, our younger generation, to go to school so that you will not suffer any humiliation from people of affluence. **Education is light of mind; he/she who has it, has a treasure.** Become educated and shine and uphold our family honour. Even if you have not had the opportunity to acquire conventional education, emulate our father by making use of your talent to make a living. Papa succeeded in life without academic qualifications and he made us proud. During the Nigerian-Biafran Civil War from 1967 to 1970, Papa was conscripted to go to war without training, while his son Ikechi was already with the Red Cross, serving on the front and helping the wounded soldiers. Through the mercy of God, he was brought home safely through the efforts of our mother and our brother-in-law, the late Mr. Nnanna Amara of Umuafor village, Orlu.

Occupation of Papa Konye

Papa's main jobs were wine tapping, farming and petty trading. In addition, he reared goats and sheep to augment his income. Papa was a very hardworking man and also engaged in harvesting crops such as palm heads, coconuts and African pears, by which he earned more money to provide for his family. When I was a child, we did not suffer lack.

Farming/Teamwork

Papa, Mama and their children formed a family team to make a success of their lives. As our parents strove to raise us, we made ardent efforts to help them. We became a strong team, doing farming activities and other chores to support our parents. We farmed, fetched water from the steam, fetched firewood from the bush, fetched fodder for our livestock and herded our sheep. We helped our mother to take commodities to the market to sell. We took turns in sweeping our compound, cooking, and washing our clothes and dishes. We did whatever we could to contribute to the upkeep of the family. Our parents played their roles well, and we played our parts well, too. All hands were on deck to build up the family. Our parents taught us to be responsible and productive and to respect, cherish and love one another, as well as our elders.

In the olden days in Igboland, polygamy was in vogue because a large family provided status, a workforce and security. An Igbo adage rightly explains it thus: a person with people weighs more than a person with wealth.

Some men marry many wives to have lots of children to contribute to the farming enterprise and the family welfare. However, in our case, Papa married just one wife, our mother, and God blessed the fruit of the womb and she gave birth to ten children. The nine surviving strong ones dealt with our farming and other responsibilities. Since our culture cannot do without our descendants, our maternal sisters, on a yearly basis, would come to assist our mother with some of the farm work to show their solidarity and respect. Likewise, on our paternal side, during harvesting of the yams, our father's closest male friends and relatives would come and help him to harvest the yams and carry them home. Our parents never hired labourers to do our farming. Rather, we, the children did return work for others as they had helped us. One of the living witnesses is Mr. Evaristus Okereke, a young man in our village who used to do return work with us. Love and respect are always reciprocal. We would arrange for one family's children to come and work for us, and next turn, we would go and work for them. It was very interesting teamwork. Our parents would cook three square meals that day to support our efforts. The meals were mainly breadfruit (ukwa), rice and fufu with a delicious soup full of meat and dried fish. This kind of teamwork **unified** our families and brought them very close to one another. Our parents represented us well, and we did all that we could to represent them well, too.

Our father did not own much land but was able to rent land during the growing season from those who had large farms. He had a large barn full of assorted yams. These yams had different names, such as jiocha, akwmba, nwoku, jiakpe, jioku, nwunyj, oke okwe, jiaga, ogbaje, jiukpo, nwanyi, erita and jink.

Papa taught us how to farm and how to be independent. He would first go by himself to clear the bushes, then he would ask us to till the soil. Our mother would plant the seedlings. The picture below shows the farming activities of the average family in Igboland.

A team effort: parents and children tilling the soil.
https://www.bing.com//images/search?view

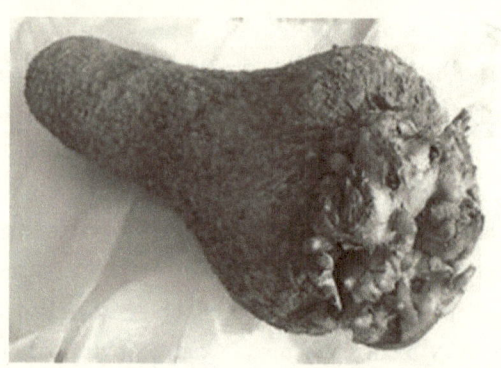

Yam tuber
https://www.bing.com//images/search?q=yam7form

Yam barn

Yam tubers for eating and planting. Papa had a large barn like this, full all the year round. His children never suffered from hunger. We enjoyed helping him build his barn.

Palm Wine Tapping

Source: https://www.nairaland.com/attachments/10140926_photogrid1567234997884jpegeba317464a6a667735ddc353af201911

Papa was in palm wine making all his life. This was his major source of income and the means by which he provided both primary and secondary education for his children. As his name Konyezuruhu implies, he was always content with what he had. He never looked into people's affairs. He never scrambled for other people's things, but when they scrambled for his, he stood tall to fight for his rights. He was okay with his own things and always strove to better himself, his wife and his children. All his focus was on how to make his children grow up to live wealthy lives as good citizens of Igboland and the entire world. Papa achieved this goal even when his children were unable to earn money to take care of him, although he enjoyed a little from Dede'm Ikechi, who started earning with his teaching career, and also from two of his daughters who had got married by then. Papa achieved his ultimate objective of ensuring that his children became good citizens. It has happened as he wished. I, the author, am a good citizen of Africa and the USA and a good resident of the United Kingdom; likewise, my nephews, nieces and cousins who live in different parts of the globe.

Ete or Apalinkwu (a Contrivance for Climbing Palm Trees)

Papa used an "ete" (apali) for climbing the oil palm trees. An ete is made of six strands of "nkoto" or plant vines about five feet long, twisted around the palm trunk and knotted together at the back of the climber. The climber gets a foot hold on the palm trunk while moving the ete up the tree trunk, step by step, until he gets near the crown of the palm tree where the palm bunches are located. He steadies himself on the ete before cutting down the palm bunch or tapping the young flowering bunch for wine. It is an expert industry, and papa was adept at it.

Papa used to climb palm trees and cut down the bunches of palm fruit like these here.
https://www.bing.com/images/search?view

Uses of the Oil Palm Tree

1. We use the palm fruits to make palm oil for cooking.
2. We use the palm oil to make local pomade (lotion).
3. We use the palm frond sheath (igbogiri) for firewood and palm frond (ogugo) for building roof rafters, making fences and staking yam vines.
4. We use the fruit fibres (abubonkwu) to make local lamp light (ederi).
5. We burn the palm bunch core fibre to ash (ngu) to make a local black soap. We also use the ash for cooking breadfruit seeds (ukwa).
6. Palm trunks are used as beams and cross beams in building houses.
7. We use the palm kernel to make palm kernel oil (ude aki) and palm kernel cake for animal feed.
8. We also use the palm frond front sheath for making ropes for tying things together in buildings and fencing and also for tethering goats.
9. The midribs of the palm's pinnate leaf are made into brooms for sweeping houses and compounds.
10. The palm leaves are used as fodder for domestic animals and poultry or as farmyard compost.
11. Our ancestors (traditional pagan worshipers) used the yellow foliage to build their shrines when making sacrifices to their gods (chi).

12. Ownership of an oil palm tree plantation is highly valued in our culture for it was the products of the oil palm tree, the palm oil and palm kernels, that were at the heart of the important commodities trade between the Europeans and Africans during the colonial era. Our ancestors grew rich from this palm oil trade, as my father, Konye, did.
13. The yellow foliage plays a significant role in our culture; when displayed on farmlands or roads, it signifies caution. Even more importantly, whenever someone commits a crime, it will be used to touch the person's body to indicate that he or she is unclean.
14. The yellow palm head on the right above is medicinal and always ripens in four market days (Eke, Orie, Afor and Nkwo). It completes its cycle in these market days before it is fully ripened. It doesn't grow at random; it is always scarce and might be found on only one or two trees in the whole town. Its name is "Ojukwu" which means beauty and healing. This is where our mother's name, Ojukwu, originated.

Kola nut tree   Kola nut seeds

 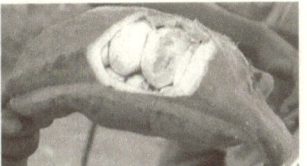

Alligator pepper   Kola nut in its shell

The Importance of Kola Nut

The kola nut tree is native to the tropical rainforests of Africa. Our father grew a few on his farm. The kola nut has a bitter flavour and is crunchy when chewed. It contains caffeine, so students who want to keep alert when studying chew, it. Kola nut is highly regarded in Igboland and other parts of Nigeria. It is used on every ceremonial occasion. In any ceremony in Igboland, if kola nut is not presented, people will raise eyebrows. It is an obligatory welcoming gesture; it shows that the visitor is warmly welcomed. It is also an expression of love and commitment. If kola nut is not presented, the visitor will wonder whether they are, indeed, welcome. Kola nut is a symbol of unity among the people. It goes along with palm wine and alligator pepper. Our celebrations are incomplete if these items are not there. In our culture, if a man offers kola nut and palm wine and people refuse them, that man is viewed as a bad man. Hence, Papa was blessed; people shared with him, drank his palm wine and ate with him. This is part of our pride. Kola nut has many uses, including medication, but I will not go into detail as I am here to exhibit the efforts of our father, Konyezuruyahu Nwadike.

Peeled and Unpeeled bitter Kola, Garden eggs, Imimi - out layer very sweet, seeds inside verry hot.
Source: WhatsApp chat 2020

In our culture, the women grow garden eggs, which are a variety of eggplant. They serve them with spiced peanut butter on every occasion, while the men present the rest. Our parents were among those who participated in these rites of kola berries and garden eggs.

Cocoa Tree

Papa Konye also cultivated a few Cocoa trees in his backyard, and he would harvest the pods and sell them in the market. Whenever there was a shortage of okra for making soup, our mother would pluck the little baby Cocoa fruits to thicken our soup for dinner. Cocoa is a very lucrative crop. Any family that has a cocoa plantation is a wealthy family and would never lack income. In Nigeria, fourteen out of thirty-six states produce cocoa in great quantities. These states are

Abia, Adamawa, Akwa Ibom, Cross River, Delta, Edo, Ekiti, Kogi, Kwara, Ogun, Ondo, Osun, Oyo and last but not least, Taraba. Our dad just cultivated a few to make ends meet. He was a man with foresight. Nothing took him unawares.

Cocoa plant Cocoa seeds
Source: https://uk.images.search.yahoo.com/search/images

Uses of Cocoa

1. It serves as a thickening agent for soups.
2. It is used in the production of chocolate, Ovaltine and coffee.
3. It is used in the making of beverages.
4. It is an ingredient of certain medications.
5. The leaves are used as compost.
6. The branches are used for fire wood.

Coconuts

My father owned a plantation of coconut palms that produced coconut fruit for sale and consumption. He also had dwarf coconut trees (Igbos call them "aki nwansh") that were easily reachable from the ground. After school, my two younger siblings, Nne'm Livy and Nna'm Bosco, and I would tiptoe around and pluck a coconut each to get the juice to put on garri porridge. We made sure that we plucked the coconuts in such a way our father would not notice their loss, and we would tidy the place up and put away all the remnants of the coconuts before he returned. We had great fun with those coconuts.

Papa also used to climb big coconut trees and pick the fruit for other people, earning money for his labour.

The Importance of the Coconut Palm

Burlil (1935) describes the coconut palm as "one of nature's greatest gift to man" because of its numerous uses. Of the more than 100 products made from coconuts, seven are important in world trade. These are:

1. Whole coconuts (tender and green, as well as dry and mature)

2. Copra: dried coconut flesh
3. Coconut oil extracted from copra or directly from the flesh
4. Coconut oil cake: the residue after the extraction of oil
5. Desiccated shredded coconut
6. Coconut skim milk and protein
7. Coir: fibre from the husk.

Coconuts provide food, oil, medicine, fibre for thatch, mats, fuel and domestic utensils. The oil is used for cooking, anointing the body (lotion), illumination, lubrication and soap-making. It plays a prominent role in the customs and folklore of many people. Coconut oil finds a number of uses in the manufacture of detergents and resins because of its melting point. Coconut stearin is a valuable confectionery fat (in cookies and ice cream). Coconut cake is used as food for cattle and poultry.

Desiccated coconut, prepared by shredding and drying the flesh, is widely used in confectionery and bakery products. Coconut milk, produced by squeezing the freshly grated meat through a sieve, is widely used in curries, sweets and other dishes. The watery juice is medicinal and a neutralizer. If one swallows poison and treats it with coconut juice, it will neutralize the action of the poison, and if one is on daily medication, one is asked not to drink the juice or eat coconut. The juice is, however, drunk as a beverage. The hard shells are used as fuel in copra kilns. Half shells are used as bowls, cups, scoops and ladles. The shells are also used for making buttons, combs, bangles and musical instruments. Coir is obtained from the fibrous husk that is removed in the preparation of copra. In Southern India, coir is made into yarn for the manufacture of mats, rugs, carpets, ropes, twine and cables. The leaves of the coconut palm are plaited and used for thatching, mats, screens, hats, and baskets. The midribs are made into brooms and baskets. The trunks are used for building and firewood.

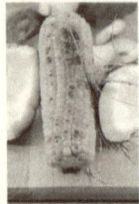  

Coconut meat goes with corn and garri, while garri goes with groundnuts (peanuts) or coconut juice. We enjoyed these during our father's time.
Source: https://uk.images.search.yahoo.com/search/images

 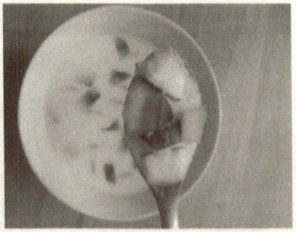

Source: https://uk.images.search.yahoo.com/search/images

African Pear Fruits

As we eat coconuts with corn and garri, we also eat these local pears with corn. After eating the outer layers of the pears, we feed the inner parts to the livestock. Similarly, when we eat the edible part of the corn, we use the cobs for firewood. One can see that God has blessed us with many good fruits and resources. Our father laboured to provide us with all of these.

Papa used to pick pear fruits like these. He also grew them for sale.
Source: https://uk.images.search.yahoo.com/search/images

Papaya

 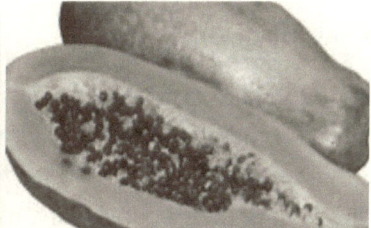

Papaya plant (Mgbimgb) and papaya fruit
Source: https://uk.images.search.yahoo.com/search/images

Papaya is a tropical tree about 20 to 30 feet tall, crowned by huge, long-stalked, deeply lobed leaves and festooned with as many as 40 or 50 football-sized fruits. The fruit of the papaya is rich in vitamins A and C, as well as riboflavin and thiamine. The vitamin C content is higher than that of oranges and strawberries. Papayas have a milky juice and black seeds; both contain papain, an enzyme used to tenderize meats. Papaya is one of the fruits our father had in his compound all the year round. We ate it a lot. It could be used in garri porridge or salads or eaten on its own. The leaves and seeds are medicinal. The leaves can be cooked with other medicinal leaves (Bitter Leaf and Utazi leaves) for curing yellow fever (jaundice). The boiled liquid is given to the patient to bathe with. We had many other plants that I cannot enumerate here. These are just to enable you to visualize what our parents had in their lifetime. They made us proud.

Raffia Palm (Ngwo)

Papa used to make raffia-thatch mats for roofing. He used these mats for mending his own roof when it leaked during the rainy season. He also sold mats to those who needed them for roofing their houses. Papa used to work round the clock to make ends meet. He would regularly stay up outside till midnight, making the raffia mats. He also extracted the twine (akwara) for ropes used for tethering goats and sheep. He made all these for domestic use and for sale. Our father was industrious and his efforts brought enlightenment to our lives.

Raffia palm tree (Ngwo)
Source: https://uk.images.search.yahoo.com/search/images

A young man making raffia-thatch mats.
Source: https://www.google.co.uk

Papa Konye used to do the same at night, working outside in the moonlight. Most often, he used a local oil lamp to help him see.

The yellow part of the raffia palm leaves is called "ashish".
Source: https://www.google.co.uk

The yellow part of the raffia palm leaves is used in producing traditional dancers' dresses for the "okorosha", "mmanwu", "ebuebu" and "okokonko" dances. It is also used for weaving local baskets such as "out." Otu are used for storing items such as clothes and raw food. Most importantly, this yellow part of the leaves was used by our ancestors to make traditional baskets in which they put sacrificial offerings to their Chi (gods). Papa used to make them as well. He was a compendium of wisdom and talents that enabled him to thrive his way to self-actualization.

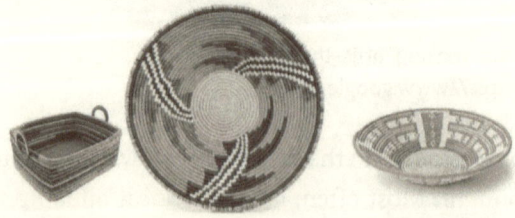

Samples of Otu

Rope (Omu or Eriri)

Source: https://uk.images.search.yahoo.com/search/images

Papa made rope out of raffia (akwara ngwo) for tethering goats and sheep and also some extra ropes which he sold in the market for money with which he bought food for his wife and children. Papa was very industrious and imparted this attitude to his children. Whatever the odds, he was equal to the occasion.

Gourds (Mbele)

In many regions of the world, calabashes or bottle gourds are classified as Lagenaria siceraria, distinct from other varieties of the cultivated gourd family known as Cucurbitaceae. They were used as domestic utensils before pottery was invented. These gourds were made into bottles, jars (mbele), bowls (agbugba), ladles (eku), spoons (ngaji), churns, cups (iko), horns (opi), musical pipes (opi), musical harps (ubo), floats for fishing nets (ibo ochokolo) and fishing hook floats (nwaogbama inchu). They are also decorated as ornamental gourds and musical instruments (sakara or oyo) and used in charms (ibo Nmanwu) or as fufu containers (agbugba nri). Mbele is a type of gourd used to store palm wine, water or oil.

A fresh gourd   Gourd spoon

Gourd (Mbele)   Eating bowl (Okwa, Agbugba)

Our father used to prepare gourds in different ways, some as eating bowls, some as drinking cups and some with lids for storing and preserving food in the kitchen. Some of the gourds were used for drinking wine, juice or water. Papa specialized in making gourds for wine-tapping. Gourds are of great value throughout Africa.

https://www.bing.com/images/search?view=

These gourds have been made into musical instruments. They give people joy when they are played. Socializing is part of our cultural heritage.

Udu-Nmanya (Earthenware Jar)

Udu-nmanya is an earthenware jar used for storing palm wine obtained from tapping oil palm or raffia palm trees. The palm wine is milk-coloured and very nutritious. The palm wine (nwanyi ogolo) is usually mixed one-to-one with water and so is made ready for drinking.

Earthenware jar (Udu)   Glass jar (Karama)   Gourd jar (Mbele)

Papa Konye used to store wine in these kinds of containers for family use and for sale. He used to provide most of the things he needed, and this attitude helped him avoid a lot of stress looking for money to buy them. Anything he could not produce himself, he bought, such as earthenware jars and glass jars. He was not a rich man but a resourceful one, capable of sustaining his family. However, he had a lot of earthenware jars from the market to enable him to preserve his wine. In Igboland, it is the men who trade in wine and kola nuts; it is solely men's business. Every morning when our Papa used to prepare the wine in a big basin, many men would sit around him in a circle. When he had finished, our father would offer each man a cup of wine to drink. Most often, there would be about five men waiting to get a free cup of wine. Then, he would pour the rest of the wine into the jars for selling. This shows how popular and generous he was. He might have stayed inside to prepare the wine and brought it out for people to buy.

Religion (Traditional Religion)

Papa was born in a polygamous and non-Christian family. He worshipped God in the original traditional religion in which God Almighty and his deities were offered animals, meat, wine, bread, vegetables, clothes, symbols of things and chalk (nzu edo and ofos). These are the same things God asked Abraham to offer to him. In fact, Mary and Joseph offered two pigeons on behalf of Jesus (Luke 2:24-28). At that time, Jesus' parents also offered their sacrifice for purification; either a pair of doves or two young pigeons was the legal requirement (from The Living Bible, Catholic edition). The colonialists called our father's religion a pagan religion although in Africa there was no such a word. African civil processes and religious processes are intertwined in such a way that every activity contains an expression of thanks to God. An example is our naming process. Almighty God is not always worshipped directly. Some honours are offered to the deities, who transmit the offerings to God Almighty. We Catholics say the litany to the Blessed Virgin Mary and Joseph. We observe the feast days of saints and ask them to intercede for us. Likewise, traditional religion offers sacrifices to Ala, Agwunsi, Ahiajioku and Amadioha, who are all deities. God empowered the deity Ala (earth god) to raise things to life and the deity Obana (river goddess) to raise fish and other things to life (c/f Genesis 1:11-12). God said, "Let the earth burst forth with every sort of grass…" (Genesis 1:20). Then God said, "Let the waters teem with fish and other life…" God even empowered man to increases and multiply (Genesis 1:28), and so, when we make babies, we are worshipping God for we are obeying his law. So did my parents obey and produced ten of us.

Papa's ancestors believed in God and worshipped God according to the original God's commandments. Remember the Jews did not know God until Moses was born in Egypt; this was the root of their religion. Moses was an Egyptian who studied all the liturgies of Egyptian religion and was initiated into all the mystical aspects of Egyptian religion, thereby qualifying to be a Pharaoh. Jesus Christ chose wine and bread as his sacrificial offerings, signifying the efficacy and authenticity of the original traditional religion. Papa feared God, lived a just and honest life and allowed all his children to be baptised in the Catholic Church. He allowed me to attend Block Rosary devotions in May and October every year. He and Mama never stopped me, even for one day. They accorded me every support I needed to practice my faith. This is the sole reason why I am what I am today – a

Catholic nun – and so this is part of what makes us proud. Thank you immensely, Papa na Mama – rest in peace.

Celebration of Ahiajioku

This is a celebration of the end of the yam harvest. Yams are harvested twice yearly. The first-harvested yams are used for celebrating iriji ofuo (ikpara Ala unwu). The king and god (Ala) celebrate the new yam festival. Then the second and final yam harvest ushers in the Ahiajoku celebration. Ahiajoku is the god in charge of farms, farming and harvest. Before, one starts farming (that is, clearing the bush), one has to offer a he-goat (nwamkpi) sacrifice (aja-oru) to god (Ahiajoku) for the crop's protection and productivity. At the end of the second harvest, offerings are made to Ahiajoku for his protection and the abundance of the crops. Chickens and food are offered. Each family has an Ahiajoku shrine in its barn. Some communities use this occasion to celebrate their annual Emumme Iriji Ala Igbo. This is the traditional religious yam festival in Igboland. At our traditional yearly festivals (Ngbo Nwanunu emume iriji na ala Igbo), all the traditional religious leaders of families would collect cockerels (oke okpa) from parents who had had sons and hens (nnekwu) from parents who had had daughters to offer as sacrifices to their highest gods, Amadioha (Chukwu

Okike Abiama or Almighty God) and Ala, the goddess. Our father, being one of these traditional leaders, would bring his cockerel (oke okpa), kola nuts, palm wine, plaited palm leaves (omunkwu) and his wife's hen (nnekwu) to offer to their gods and the ancestors. Our mother would prepare onunu or abubo – yam mashed with palm oil and bread fruit meal (ukwa) – and would give these to our father to offer to their gods (chi) and the ancestors. On this occasion, I used to stand behind Papa in his shrine whenever he was presiding over the sacrifices. I loved to listen to his incantations to his god (chi) and to the ancestors. He used to ask God for favours and interventions on behalf of his family, friends and well-wishers. These are his invocations:

> "Please, Eternal Father, our leader, we invoke you; let it be done according to your good will. We call on you in the name of our ancestors of times immemorial; those who had earned illustrious estates and enjoyed them. We thank you for those who were self-realized and had great households and alacrity.

We Beseech You to Endow Us with the Following

Good health, long life, and wisdom
Good estates and good homes
Good fathers and good mothers

Good brethren and good friends
Good wives and good children
Good occupations and good savings
Good wealth and good money
Let it be all festivities and rejoicings
Let our words be delightfully interesting
Let those who meet the parrot rejoice with it
Let those who meet the eagle rejoice with it.

For it is good upbringing to give credit to whom it is due. We give you our praises for your benevolence to us by offering to you our sweet-smelling gifts for all your blessings from our ancestors through Jesus. Thank you for making our crops grow successfully and mature for harvest."

He always said, "I never planned any evil against anybody and let nobody plan any evil against me and my families." He would add, "This year's harvest was not too plentiful so let next year's one be more fruitful," meaning, in Igbo, *nke afoa ebudibu, nke afo ozo ga aka*. He would then kill the cockerels and the hens and sprinkle their blood on the altar of the shrine. Mashed yam and breadfruit meal were also placed on the shrine for the ancestors to eat. Papa would give me the chickens to send to our mother to prepare for meal. From Papa, I learned how to pray by wishing people well. Papa never wished anybody evil; that was the reason why God blessed him and he was able to raise his children well, even in the eye of the storms. His Chi-God was with him all through life. God rewarded him by choosing his daughter to be the first Reverend Sister in our noble village of Ndiowerre, which had had neither Reverend Father nor Reverend Sister since its creation. We thank you for your abundant love for us.

Education

Papa Konye was not educated according to modern educational convention but was skilled in the local industries and could make tools (for example, the ete or apali) for industrial processes. He knew the value of conventional education and was an advocate of it for he got all his children educated. Here is my position on this. When he wanted to educate his first son, Dede'm Ikechi, people discouraged him because of his low-income status. Nevertheless, he ignored them and saw him through his secondary education. Dede'm Ikechi finished his education with flying colours and later became a popular instructional teacher. He also afforded my other siblings both primary and secondary education.

Here is another testimony concerning our father's education of his children. During my primary school days, my younger sister, Oluaka-Ngozi Livina, would come home from school and give Papa long lists of our school requirements. He would ride his bicycle (igwe) to our local market called Ahia Ugwumabiri (Orlu Daily Market) and buy all the school materials, including books, for us. He would not allow us to be sent home from school for being unable to pay our school fees. He always ensured we paid our school fees ahead of time. He gave all his children equal opportunity, support and encouragement for a good education. I believe his wish was fulfilled. His ardent empowerment, motivation and encouragement made me strive higher in academic pursuit and self-actualization.

Papa, I am documenting this to show my appreciation to you and Mama. Your efforts were not in vain. We attained the goal you set before us, as you expected. We are proud of you. We followed in your footsteps and those of our mother, who used to say to us, "My children, *agwo aghaghi imu ihe toro ogologo*," meaning "like begets like." I believe in this wise saying of Mama's because all my siblings were and are as hardworking as our parents. We are prudent and proud of our family and are far-reaching in all our endeavours. When I was a student in the USA, I applied Papa and Mama's attitudes towards success in anything I embarked on. Come rain or shine, I would be out there striving to achieve my goal. One of their common inspirational proverbs is: "A child of a poor man is never a fool; he/she is always wise; hence, a poor man's child is always careful and not lavish." In Igboland of Biafra, this is the adage *umu m nwa, nwa ogbenye anaghi awusa nkpuru ano*.

Our father left a great legacy for all his children. He never misled us or allowed anybody to mislead him. He was independent. He always advised us to bring home and show him or Mama any gift from anybody so that they would be able to thank the person. He always discouraged us from gourmandising as he said, "My children, *umu orimara butere akpiri udele.*" Too much eating causes guzzling (akpiri) like a vulture. Then he would reprimand us and would never offer us that particular food in order to discipline us. He made us to be contented with what we had. Papa, like our Mama, taught us forgiveness. Take, for example, the land dispute he had with his neighbours. In all that time, he never fought anybody and he still got along with them. This is how it should be whenever we have an issue with anybody. We should borrow a leaf from our parents' book and forgive one another and forge ahead. Remember, life is very short. Why worry ourselves unnecessarily?

Papa's character

Gentle: Whatever the situation, one would never see or hear Papa talking loudly or reacting violently. Instead, he would remain calm. Papa was a respectful, kind-hearted and compassionate man.

Industrious: Papa was not the talking type but rather a man of action. He worked tirelessly and relentlessly with his wife, Ojukwu, to raise their children and trained them well, both spiritually and academically.

Faithful: Papa was faithful to his wife till death parted them. He lived a clean life.

Generous: He always shared what he had with people if anybody was in need.

Truthful: He always maintained the truth, even at the risk of his life.

Fearless: Each time neighbours wanted to take his land and palm trees, he never feared them. Despite being alone among them, he had always his Chi (Almighty God) on his side that protected him and led him.

Determined: Papa Konye was always focused on his daily tasks.

Things Papa Used when He was Living on Earth

Mud House: Papa built and lived in a mud house with four rooms and one kitchen. He lived there with his wife, who gave birth to ten of us. We all lived very close together, shared with one another and learned from one another. The mud house needed high maintenance because its roof was built of raffia-straw mats. Each rainy season, the roof would deteriorate and Papa would make straw mats to repair it. Mama and the girls were in charge of mopping the walls and the floors with water to keep the house clean and cool.

Land: Papa had a few pieces of land, and he succeeded in training his children to use it.

Bicycle: Our father had a strong, black bicycle that he rode all his life. He always maintained it till his last day on earth.

Papa owned, enjoyed and rode on a bike like this one throughout his life.

Double Barrel Gun: Papa had a long double barrel gun which he used to hunt animals. He hunted as a hobby. Once he'd sighted a suitable animal, he would shoot without missing. He was a true marksman. During the Nigerian-Biafran Civil War, our father used to hide his gun in an unknown place that no one would dream of. I was the only one in the family who knew where he hid it. Papa was meticulous, and he imparted this quality to his children. He used to do things quietly and successfully. I emulated this aspect of him a lot. People often see me as someone who is not responsible, but when they see my performance, they marvel, as they marvelled at Papa's success in his endeavours.

Big Knife (Nma Oge) or Machete

Papa had also a big sharp knife called "nma oge" that he used for cutting down thick forest to make way for farming. He maintained this knife well and never allowed the children to handle it because it was too sharp.

Obi: An obi is a stick made out of the straight part of a young plant. It is about five feet long and has one end trimmed to a sharp point for digging big holes in the ground. Big sticks can be put in these holes as stakes for training yam vines.

Mbazu: A mbazu is like an obi, but instead of having a sharpened end, it has a flattened end for uprooting yams during harvesting. Papa used an mbazu to harvest his yams.

Ube: An ube is similar to a mbazu and is used for the same purpose.

Ete: Papa used an ete (apali) for climbing palm trees (see above where wine-tapping was discussed). Only experts can use an ete to climb trees.

Biafra Suit: Papa Konye had and wore only one suit in his lifetime. It was called his Biafra suit. He always wore it when he went to a family party. He also put this suit on whenever friends invited him and his wife to festival celebrations.

Leather Shoes: He had a pair of leather shoes that he used to wear during festival celebrations. Papa was very careful and economical.

Wristwatch: He also had a wristwatch that he wore. He knew how to manage and regulate his time. I inherited this talent from him. He was never late in any of his schedules. He never disappointed people for any appointment or kept them waiting.

Easy Chair: Papa had one easy chair that he used throughout his life. He always kept it neat.

Table/Chairs: Papa had a dinner table and some chairs. We used the table for writing and reading our books. He also had two small serving tables, one for him and one for us.

Okpo-Okpo: This is a large family bed made of bamboo sticks that every child in the house slept on. One side of it was where cooking pots and kitchen materials were kept. Papa built it by himself for the family to use.

Mkpoko: This is a kind of store room where treasures are kept. Papa used to store our valuable goods there.

Uko: This is a place for drying fresh meat, food, corn and seeds for the next planting season. In the olden days, every family in Igboland had one for preserving things for future use.

Clay Pots: Papa also furnished our back yard with clay pots for drinking water. Children fetched water and poured it into the pots. During the rainy season, the rain water would fill the pots directly from the heavens. Our family was self-sufficient and we lacked nothing.

More About My Father, Konye

Papa's last day on earth was the 14th of January, 1980. He died on a Monday at 7 am. Papa, after he had been conscripted during the Nigerian-Biafran Civil War, became ill. He started suffering from asthma after being in the bush for months. He lived with this ill health for years before he broke down. However, his ill health never prevented him from doing his daily activities. He working determinedly till his last day on earth. On the evening before he passed on, he wanted to go and tap his wine, but our mother refused to allow him to do that. On the 12th of January, 1980, I was helping Dede'm Ikechi to tie Papa's yams on the barn sticks. At one point, I went to see Papa in his parlour where he was resting on his easy chair. I gave him a banana to eat. I was concerned about his health and started soliloquizing. Dede'm Ikechi came in from the backyard and heard me talking to myself. He asked me who I was talking to, and I told him I was not talking to anybody – the person had gone.

The spirit told me something about our father's condition, but I could not comprehend it. On Sunday, the 13th of January, after Mass at St. Peter's Church Amike, my friend, Lucy Ogoeze, asked me to accompany her to the Marist Brothers of the Schools compound to see the late Reverend Brother Bernard Okofar. When we arrived, I stayed in their little religious articles shop while Lucy went up to see the Reverend Brother. When she had finished, she met me there and we left. When we reached home, behold, one of the brothers by the name of Rev. Br. Richard Okofor drove into our compound with his driver. I ran to hug him, but he ignored me. He said to me, "My daughter, I am not happy with you. Did you come to our compound today?" I answered, "Yes, Brother, I did." Then he asked, "Why did you stay away while only Lucy came in?" I explained to him that it was Lucy who had wanted to see Rev. Br. Bernard. He said, "Okay, I was just wondering why you had stayed outside." Then he asked me about my father. I told him that he was sick inside. He went and saw him. When he came out, he called me, took me aside and said, "My daughter, if your father lasts another week, he will live longer." Then he told me that he had talked to him about baptism and he'd agreed to receive it. Rev. Br. Richard promised to come with our parish priest on Monday, the 14th of January, to baptise him. As God willed it, I was the one who baptised him instead. One strange thing was that my mother never knew the arrangement between the Reverend Brother and me. While we were with Papa in his room, my mother asked me, "Nne'm, have you baptised your father?" I went immediately and got blessed water. I named him John and then baptised him in the name of the Father and of the Son and of the Holy Spirit. Papa lingered awhile. He was lying on his side, and at one point, he propped himself up and tried to draw back one of his legs. My mother said to me, "Nne, hold your father's leg and don't allow him to bend it." Papa went to sleep peacefully in the Lord at 7 am on Monday, the 14th of January, 1980. There was no struggling nor any pain. I took Dede'm Ikechi's bike, which I used to go to school at Ihioma Girls, and rode to let the Reverend Brothers know that my dad had expired. The Rev. Br. Bernard Okafor went to my school and reported it to my principal.

During his funeral, many of the Marist Brothers came to offer their condolences. I am documenting this to show you vividly the kind of life our father lived and the type of people he associated with. Papa and his family never associated with bad people. Papa used to welcome the Brothers warmly whenever they visited us. Mama, though a non-Christian, knew the importance of baptism and motivated me to baptise Papa. What made her have that trust in me is still a great mystery. My association with Mama always makes me think that she saw something significant in me. She trusted me so much, and this trust caused me to be very careful in my daily activities and relationships with people. Mama was the ultimate pride of our family. According to a former USA President, there are two kinds of success:

> *"One is the very rare kind that comes to the man who has power to do what no one else can do. That is genius. But the average man who wins what we call success is not a genius. He is a man who has merely the ordinary qualities like others, but who has developed those ordinary qualities to a more than ordinary degree."*
>
> - Theodore Roosevelt
> www.livinglifefully.com/meditations/
> medmar6.htm
> www.worldfuturefund.org/
> Documents/maninarena.htm

Mama Ojukwu Monica Agim Konye Nwadike

Mama Ojukwu was born in 1914 to the family of Agim Okafor Nwaugbala of Umuokwaraibekwe, Umuokwarairobe Umsasa, Uzoubi Autonomous Community. She was the third child of Agim Okafor Nwaugbala and Nneenyidiyi Ojiobianu. Her parents had five children, namely, Titus, Adaeriri, Ojukwu, Augustina and Theresa. Mama was about five feet tall. She was fair in complexion, with black hair and deep brown eyes. She was a beautiful, warm-hearted woman who always had a smile on her face. Our mother was hardworking and followed her mother to many markets such as Orie Ugwu, Orie Amaroaku and Eke Ututu to trade their wares. She was keen to go to school, so her father sent her to school, but one day, her teacher flogged her for being late. She went home and told her father, and her father withdrew her from school. That was the end of her academic career, which she regretted all her life. However, her parents gave her sound training at home. Her father always allowed her to sit by his side whenever he had important meetings or deliberations so that she would listen and remind him of anything he might have forgotten. This opportunity gave my mother wonderful inspiration and wisdom. It empowered her to talk figuratively, using idioms, proverbs and body language to approve or disapprove of good or wrong actions. When her senior sister, Adaeriri, got married to my uncle, Chief Mgbaja Nwadike of Ndiowerre village, Mama Ojukwu constantly visited her. All this time, she did not escape the eagle eyes of our uncle. He saw her as a promising wife for his half-brother, Konye, a loyal, hardworking, respectful, outgoing man, whom she eventually married. As a result, Adaeriri and our mother married into the same family of Nwadike. We and Dada Adaeriri's eight children used to go together to our maternal home every year for new yam festivals and other important ceremonies. We ate and enjoy together.

Mama, like Papa, lived a fulfilled life. She had everything an average mother should have to raise her children. She was self-reliant and independent. Neighbouring women used to come to her to borrow a few vegetables and other food stuff for cooking. She was always hospitable. She spoke her mind, but she would always ask people for pardon if she had wronged them. She never bore grudges and easily forgave people who had offended her. She would always say, "Leave everything for Chukwu Okike Abiama (Almighty God)."

Our mother regretted her lack of schooling and vowed that in her next coming, she would embrace Western education. She made sure that her children acquired a good education, both domestically and academically. Her support for education gave the family NCE teachers, a Doctor of Philosophy Psychology, a Master of Science Business Administration (MSBA), and a Bachelor of Science Computer Information Systems (BSCIS). She also encouraged her grandchildren to be educated: "I would not allow you to be like me who did not go to school."

Our mother was a woman of strong character. She was very energetic and always ready to help solve people's problems. With her strong support for her husband, they were able to support others who sought their help. They lent people money in exchange for land for farming. Like our father, our mother hated injustice and cherished truth.

She always wanted her children to tell the truth, no matter the situation. She was generous and received all those that came to her. From our parents, we acquired the spirit of forgiveness. We learnt a lot about tolerance, forgiveness, and forgetting ugly experiences during our childhood days that have been put aside, and we are living harmoniously with one another.

Although our mother was born in a non-Christian family and married into a "pagan" family, she encouraged her daughter to become a Sister in the Congregation of The Holy Family Sisters of the Needy. Because of this, she decided to join the Catholic faith. Although a non-Christian, each time she gave birth, she took the baby to the church for baptism. Mama was a woman of great character, a real genius, a loving mother without comparison, a great psychologist and a natural philosopher. She was a woman of wisdom and insight who spoke to her children through her body language, such as using her eyes, twisting her mouth, or waving her hands, and using proverbs. I have described this aspect of her in detail in my other book, *Ancestral Legacy of Family Counselling*. She used positive or negative songs to affirm or disapprove of an action. Mama was a compendium of determination, endurance, compassion, industry, forgiveness, peace-making, understanding, prayerfulness, gentleness, generosity and patience.

Mama's Conversion to Christianity

Mama, Ojukwu, was wholeheartedly converted to the Catholic faith in 1987 when she visited Oshogbo to babysit Mrs. Engineer Onyeajuwa Livina Ngozi's first child. On the first Sunday, they attended Sunday Mass, leaving her behind and locking the doors. She joined the family at morning and night prayers. Sometimes, she would call for prayer. The following Saturday night, she got her clothes ready. Before Livy and her husband got out of bed on Sunday morning, she was dressed and ready for the service. That day, she made up her mind to be a Christian. When she returned East, she enrolled for catechism classes at Holy Trinity Cathedral Parish Church Orlu. When she passed the oral test conducted by the Marist Brothers, she was baptised and was called Monica, the name I gave her. I brought four names for her to choose from: Magdalene, Agatha, Elizabeth and Monica. Immediately, she chose Monica and was happy to be called by it. One significant thing about our mother's conversion to Christianity is that she had told me that she would become a Christian when her mind accepted it; nobody should convert her to Christianity. She said this because the Legionaries from our church used to visit her and preach at her to become a Christian. I used to invite the Marist Brothers to preach to her, but it all fell on deaf ears. The late Rev. Br. Richard Okafor and other younger Brothers used to visit her for the same purpose, but she refused and said to me, "Nne'm Rosa, I will go to Church when my mind accepts it." One day, she sent Dada'm Henrietta and Mr. Anthony Madueke to visit me in the Convent at Nekede to inform me that she had started going to church. She added, according to their disclosure, "Nnne'm, stop crying, I am now a Christian." As an adult, she became a communicant the day she was baptised. When she was active, she hardly missed morning masses. She was later confirmed. Being among her brother-in-law, her daughter and their new-born baby motivated her to go to church. This proves the wise saying; one good turn deserves another. The presence of the new-born baby brought blessing to us.

Our mother was a great dancer in her women's dancing group in the village. In the picture below, Mama is the person in the front-line dancing with a cow's tail. This was her last dancing activity on earth before her passing into eternity at the ripe old age of ninety-five at 4.45 pm on the 12th of November, 2009, at Imo State University Teaching Hospital, Umuna, Orlu.

Mama in Positive Mood during a Village Dancing Display

Mama used to be the number one dancer in the line during the Ayoroyo-Ayoroyo group dance in our village. Igbos say, *egwu amuru na nwata ukwu ejiegba ya na eru ala*. This implies that a dance that one learnt during childhood is characterized by the fact that the dancer is able to bend gracefully in rendering it, which is not possible for a person who learnt it in old age. When Mama danced, she was given the name "Machine Oke Aku." This title is also as a result of her giving birth to numerous children and grandchildren. Later, I will list the names and of our parents' grandchildren and great-grandchildren.

Titular Names Depicting Her Prowess and Her Womanly Attributes

Ojukw Saraugo	- A precious woman
Mamakukwu	- The big mother
Machine Oke aku	- A woman of wealth
Ojukwu Biafra	- Nwanyi Biafra
Nwanyi aka ruru n'ihe obuna	- A woman of privilege
Nneoma	- A good mother
Nwanyi amuma	- A great psychologist
Odoba nwanyi okaa ome	- A natural philosopher

Some of Mama's Possessions

Okunri (Earthenware plate)

Clay jug for water

Clay pot for food storage

Clay pot and bowls for serving food Wooden spoon
https://uk.images.search.yahoo.com/search/images

Iteigwe: In Igboland, only wealthy women could afford this kind of big iron pot. Women who did not have these kinds of pots used to go to their neighbours to borrow them whenever they had celebrations that required them to cook large quantities of food. Mama had two big pots like this with lids, and her neighbours borrowed them from her on important occasions.

Iteigwe (Iron Pot): The kind of big iron pot Mama used for cooking.

Ekwu-igwe: Mama had an ekwu-igwe, an iron stand for supporting the pot on the fire when cooking. The picture shows a cooking stand and a big frying pot. Mama had these kinds of households items for cooking and frying garri.

Ekwu-igwe   Ite Mmiri (Clay pots for water)   Ite Mmiri

Mama had some clay pots like these in our backyard for drinking water. https://www.amazon.co.uk/s?k=Igboland+clay+pots&i=kitchen&ref=nb_sb_noss

Ikwe (Mortar)　　Odu (Wooden pestle)　　Okwa

Ikwe (Mortar): This was a big wooden mortar used in pounding foo-foo. It was also used for pounding palm fruits for oil processing.

Odu **(Pestle):** This was a long wooden stick, 3 feet long, used for pounding the foo-foo in the mortar. They are still in use in our present era.

Okwa (Small mortar): An okwa is a small mortar for grinding things such as pepper and onions.

Nma Ekwu (Old kitchen knife)

Nma Ekwu (Kitchen Knife): Women use nma ekwu to peel yams and cocoyam, cut up vegetables and meat, and collect foo-foo together in a mortar so that it appears well-moulded.

Wooden chair

The List of Household Items Our Mother Used

1. Clay jug for drinking water
2. Clay pot for food storage
3. Clay plate for serving food
4. Clay plates for eating food
5. Wooden spoon for stirring and dishing food.
6. Gourd spoon for eating food
7. Iteigwe (iron pot) for cooking food
8. Ekwuigwe (iron stand) for a pot stand
9. Ite Mmiri (clay pot) for water storage
10. Ikwe (big wooden mortar) for pounding food, etc.
11. Odu (wooden pestle) for pounding food
12. Okwa (small mortar) for grinding pepper, etc.
13. Nmaekwu (kitchen knife) for cutting vegetables, meat, etc.
14. Wooden chair

Hoe (Ogu): The hoe (ogu) is for tilling the soil. Mama Ojukwu had a lot of hoes like the one in the drawing for our family farming. We produced all the food we ate – yams, cocoyam, cassava and vegetables. Mama only went to market to purchase fish and meat. However, sometimes our elder brother, the late Dede'm Ikechi, went to the stream and caught fish for us.

https://www.bing.com/search?q=african+farming+hoes&qs=n&form=

Food Mama grew or Prepared

Ukwa (Breadfruit): The fruit of the breadfruit tree is very nutritious and rich in protein. It undergoes a long process before one can make food from it. It is good food for diabetic patients.

Ukwa (Breadfruit tree), Peeled breadfruit seeds, Cooked breadfruit

"Ukwa is a traditional meal that is commonly eaten by the Igbo people of South-Eastern Nigeria. The botanical name of this food is Treculia Africana while the English name is African breadfruit. Ukwa can be made into a porridge delicacy or it can be fried and eaten with palm kernel or coconut."
Source:https://www.bing.com/
search?q=Nigerian+porridge+breadfruit+food

Ede (Cocoyam plants)   Indian cocoyam   Red cocoyam
Bing.com/search?=cocoyam&qs=&form

Ede (Cocoyam): Mama, just like her contemporaries, had a big barn for her cocoyams. We never lacked food all the year round. In Igboland, cocoyams and cassava are the major crops grown by the women. Any woman who does not have plenty of these vegetables is regarded as lazy.

Plantains and Bananas: Most Igboland women grow these plants. Mama Ojukwu grew them as a source of income and to feed her family. Both Papa and Mama were responsible human beings and role models of their era.

Plantain plants and fruit
https://www.bing.com/images/search?q=plantain%20plantation%20farming&qs=AS&form=

Banana plants and fruit
Bing.com/images/search?q=banana&q=n&form=QBR&sp=

Ona (yampi): Ona is a type of yam, a yellow tuber, very sweet when cooked. It looks like an Irish potato but bigger. Yampi is mainly found in Igboland, but not all the tribes grow them. My mother grew them annually.

Ona (Yampi) Red oil goes with yampi
https://www.bing.com/images/search?q=yampi&qs=n&form=QBIR&sp=-1&pq=yampi&sc=8

Cassava plant
Bing.com/images/search?q=cassava&qs=n&form

Cassava Roots (Jiapu): Mama had two kinds of cassava, namely, Nwaedeocha and Aburuerie. Cassava cultivars are divided into two major groups, recognized as bitter and sweet. The sweet cassavas are grown for food while the bitter type, which has a higher starch content, is cultivated for industrial purposes. Cassava is a staple food for millions of people, and Africa is the world's highest cassava producer. Garri is made from cassava. Cassava roots contain hydrocyanic acid and need to be detoxified before consumption. Cassava roots are also used as livestock feed.

Jiapu (Cassava tubers)   Tapioca sliced with peanuts

Eberebe Akpu (Tapioca): Eberebe akpu is sliced cassava. One has to cook it before slicing and soak it in water overnight. It can be eaten with peanuts, coconut and palm kernels. Mama used all these ingredients in her kitchen.

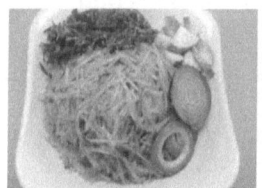 

Sliced cassava dish Sliced oil bean seed
Source: https://uk.images.seach.yahoo.com/search.images

Mothers prepare this dish differently according to their local tradition. This picture is an example of what my mother used to prepare for her family and friends. It contains sliced eberebe akpu (tapioca) mixed with red oil, onions, salt, a seasoning cube (ogiri), pepper, sliced oil-bean seeds, African garden eggs and breadfruit meal. It is delicious.

Oil-Bean Seeds

Source: https://uk.images.search.yahoo.com/search.images

Papa had a big oil-bean tree in his compound. Every year he harvested them for sale and consumption. Mama seldom bought them from the market. The seed pods are used for firewood. Children make them into toy shoes. I remember wearing them for fun. We had a happy childhood and are ever grateful to our parents.

Read through this and then begin to value your mother.

"Nobody has your back like your mama...
Love her while she is still alive.

You can never find a better friend than your mother,
So, respect her, cherish her and love her while you can.
She could be gone one day, and you will never find anyone like her.

A mother is always a mother.
She never stops worrying about her children even when they are all grown and have children of their own.

Father retires at 60,
Mother never retires.
She works for her children.
She looks after her grandchildren.

She looks after everyone.
Everyone retires,
But Mother never retires.

A mother is the only
person who carries you
for 9 months in her belly,
3 years in her arms, and forever in her heart.

Mother
Nobody can replace her.
Nobody can do half the things she does, or has done,
for you.
No matter where she is –
In Heaven or here on earth –
there is nothing like a mother's love.

The older I grow, the
More I realize that my
mother was my best friend.

A mother may be
"Educated" or "Uneducated" but she is the "Best
Guide" and "Last Hope" in the world
whenever you fail in your life.

A mother is she who can
take the place of all
others but whose place no one else can take.

A mother is the only person on earth
who can divide her love
among 10 children and each child still has all her love.

A mother is your first friend,
your best friend,
your forever friend.

Home is where your
Mom is.

Definition of Mother:
The greatest
Unconditional and infinite love we will ever
experience in our
existence...

A mother is someone
who will always support you
when you need it.
I believe in love at first
Sight because I've been
loving my mom since I

opened my eyes.

Dear Mom,
Because of you, I am
what I am today.
Thank you. I love you.

Call your mother.
Tell her you love her.
Remember you're the
only person who knows
what her heart sounds
like from the inside.

A man loves his
sweetheart the most,
his wife the best, but
his mother the longest.

Love Your Mother!
The most beautiful
person on this earth.
Our best critic, yet our
Strongest supporter.

Sourced from WhatsApp chat
January 28, 2020

Ikechi Sylvester Konye
His Greatness and Achievements

When I had a vision to write a book, I contacted my elder brother, Dede'm Ikejiofor, to give me some info about himself and our family. Accordingly, he provided me with information about our family origin and wrote about himself as follows:

> *"Personal Names:*
> *Born to Konye Nwadike family of Ndiowerre, Orlu, Town.*
> *Our parents gave me the name Ikechi (God's power).*
> *Nwadike family head - late Mgbaja Nwadike gave me the name Ikejiofor.*
> *Late Akarusi Agim of Umusasa Umuna, Orlu, gave me the name Ofojiogu.*
> *My father's mother gave me the name Jeremiah.*
> *All these names I cherish today as often as I think of them. When I joined the Catholic church, at baptism I took the name Sylvester.*
> *During the greater part of my football and running days I enjoyed the names Oganamkpa and VC10."*

By the late Mr. Ikechi Sylvester Konye,
Oganamkpa VC10
Written in 2010 Passed on in 2011.

Dede'm Ikechi was born on the 16th of June, 1947. He was the first of ten children born to our parents, Konye and Ojukwu. He was given different names by our parents, paternal parents, maternal parents, and elders, according to circumstances surrounding his birth. He was named **Ikechi** by my parents, which means the "power of God" because they believed that it was not in their power that they were able to conceive him. **Ikejiofor** was given to him by our father's half-brother, Uncle Chief Mgbaja Nwadike, and means the "holder of family title" because he was the first child and a son. **Ofojiogu** was given to him by our maternal uncle, Papa Akarusi Agim, and means "authority has righteousness to act". **Jeremiah** was given to him by my father's mother, Mama **Ogoma,** and means "prophet of God" as she had anticipated that a baby boy would be born.

Dede'm Ikechi chose Sylvester as his name during his baptism as a legitimate member of the Roman Catholic Church. **Oganamkpa** and VC10 were also given to him by his schoolmates when he excelled on the football field and in track and field events. He was also an excellent flute and trumpet player in the school band at Ojike Memorial Secondary School, Orlu, and at Bishop Shanahan Training College, Orlu.

Ikechi was loved and cherished by his elders, friends and siblings. Papa and Mama were proud of him for being their first son and a responsible young man. In Igboland, every first male child is given a lot of honour.

We, his siblings, used to address him as **Dede-e,** and I particularized him and used to address him as **Dede'm. Dede-e** means elder brother, while dede'm means my own elder brother. In Igboland- Biafra land, we call our elder brothers Dede-e to show our respect due to them as our elders. And we address our older sisters as **Dada,** also as a mark of respect. We were taught early in life that younger siblings must respect and address their elders as dede or dada. This kind of relationship brought love and concord among the siblings and their parents.

Our first nephew, Chinedozie (now Rev. Fr. Leonard Dim), started calling Ikechi **Dedeukwu'm,** meaning "**my big brother,**" and his siblings followed suit. As respect is reciprocal, Dede'm Ikechi used to address each of us as **nwanne'm,** meaning my own brother or sister, and he addressed our nephews and nieces as **nwa-nwa**, meaning children of my sisters or brothers or daughters. To reinforce my position on the respect due to our elders, I quote Harris Uchenna Nwachukwu:

> *I addressed my older brother as Dede Monday throughout his life. The word "Dede" (sometimes shortened to Dee) means "an older brother" or an older male. The Ngwa teaches respect from the early stages of life. A younger sibling must address*

his/her elder as "dede," or "dada" for an "older sister" or older female.
- Justin Harris Uchenna Nwachukwu
From There To Here
A Journey of Hopes and Dreams 2012 (p. 28)

The above quotation from Dr. Justin Harris Uchenna Nwachukwu shows that one's elders are highly respected in our culture throughout Igboland. We don't compromise on this issue. Dede or Dada is beyond respect; they also mean beloved elders – the ones we cherish. Though born in a non-Christian (pagan) family, dede'm Ikechi became a devout Christian with the support of our parents. He used to serve at Mass and was the secretary of his church group for many years. He was loved by his priests and parishioners. Our village women called him a man more beautiful than a woman. A peaceful, gentle dove.

Home Training: From the forms of greeting described above, one can infer the kind of training the Konye family gave their children and the legacy handed down the generations. Unfortunately, as I wrote in *The Ancestral Legacy of Family Counselling,* television, the Internet, Facebook, Viber, and WhatsApp are having an unwelcome influence on our children. Parents' basic home training of their children is therefore crucial.

In dede'm Ikechi's case, being the first child of Konye, he learnt good behaviour from our parents, and as we grew up, we followed in his footsteps. When he was a little child, our parents used to talk to him with sign language. Being sensible and smart, he understood any sign made to him. Dede'm Ofojiogu was a respectful, honest, gentle but strong-willed man and an honourable teacher. His yes was always yes, and his no was always no, just like our parents. One couldn't outwit or beat him. He was a man of conscience and great endurance. He was a truthful man, and most of his mates admired him for that. Farming, which he inherited from his parents, was his occupation. Like father, like son. Our parents mentored him well in farming, and we, his siblings, joined him when we were old enough. Papa also taught him how to climb certain trees. Dede'm Ikechi even did domestic work. He used to sweep our compound, fetch water from the stream, cook food, fetch fodder for our livestock and take our sheep to the bush to graze.

Peer Group: When Dede'm was growing up, he associated fully with the other boys his age, and he was loved by all. His mates used to go to the stream down the hill to catch fishes and crabs. They formed a team that swept the village square every week. In the village square, there were many mango trees that produced fruit every year. Nobody touched the fruit when it was ripe except these young men who used to sweep the square. When the fruit was ready to harvest, the boys would beat their gong for all of them to assemble to pick the fruit. Then they would share the mangos among themselves and take them home to share with their families. Young men were of good repute and in solidarity with each other then. Everybody felt free and happy. They used to go to the bush to hunt animals from their dens. Every weekend, we looked forward to eating bush meat, fish and crabs. When they killed the big bush rats, they would come either to our compound or someone else's compound to roast them and shared them among themselves. They rotated it so as to include everybody.

They also used to do "Operation keep your street clean." This included both boys and girls. As they cleaned the street, they would harvest some yams and cocoyams from every farm they passed. They picked the vegetables in a reasonable manner so as not to hurt the owners. The owners respected this as tradition and a reward for their good efforts. At the end of the exercise, they took all the yams and cocoyams to Mr. Okwaraugochukwu's compound to cook them. Mr. Okwaraugochukwu would provide them with a big pot to cook them because their activities demonstrated love and community spirit. These young men and women exhibited unity and teamwork. Later Mr. Okwaraugochukwu played his record player, called a gramophone. The young men and women would gather in his corridor, dancing happily without abusing each other. The young men would dress in benzua trousers and Torpedo shoes and had afro hair, while the girls would wear long gowns and stretched their afro hair. They looked modest and smart.

Football: Dede'm was always keen on getting involved in what others were doing that would enhance the progress of the community. He was a member of our village football club as well as his school football club. He was at one time the team coach. He was also a member of our village Youth Association, as well as Orlu Town Youth Association.

Primary School: Dede'm Ikechi's childhood dream was to be an educated man. Our parents were not educated according to English standards but they knew the value of education and always advocated the importance of education to all around them. They promised any of us who were interested an education beyond secondary level. Our parents allowed Ikechi to acquire the sound education of his heart's desire. He was enrolled in primary school at Practising School 1, Orlu Local Government, Imo State. During his schooling, he always obtained excellent results and came first in his various classes. His teacher, the late Mr. Francis Ojuike, encouraged him to proceed to higher education, which his parents managed to finance.

Secondary School: Dede'm Ikechi enrolled in Ojuike Memorial Secondary School, Orlu, for a secretarial course. At the completion of his studies, he was awarded a diploma with distinction. With his administrative skills, he decided not to be a teacher but rather to look for a secretarial appointment. Being a poor man's child, he struggled to secure a job. He sought a secretarial position for two years but to no avail. Eventually, Lady Theresa Agu, our mother's immediate younger sister (nee Agim), counselled him to reverse his decision and embark on a teaching career. He took her advice, and Papa and Mama were very supportive. They made an arduous effort to send him to Bishop Shanahan College, Orlu. Having completed his studies, he became involved in teaching for many years.

Bishop Shanahan College: Dede'm Ikechi commenced his teacher's training and at last became successful. At the college, he participated in all the school plays, as well as football, high jump, javelin and sprint races, and he performed in the school band and the march-past. These activities earned him the names **Oganamkpa and VC10.** He was named **Oganamkpa** because he was a good goal scorer; no matter where the ball was, he would control it and score a goal. He was named **VC10** as a result of his outstanding performance on the track. One could observe here the crucial influence and expert advice from one of our aunts that inspired Ikechi in his academic pursuits. Lady Theresa exhibited here our ancestral pride. She is our mother's immediate young sister and an educator. She is full of wisdom and insight. She keeps track of our all-ascendant families and always makes sure all our youngsters are progressing well.

Achievements: Once Ikechi started teaching, he used his salary to purchase a bicycle for transport. As he progressed, he was able to purchase a Suzuki motorcycle to travel faster. He bought a stereo record player that gave us music and entertainment. He demolished Papa's old house and built a new bungalow with eight rooms. He kept on encouraging us younger ones in our education. He assisted Dede'm Cordelia in her secondary school education and in her teacher training. He was also involved partially in my education, both primary and secondary. The most significant thing he did in my life was sharing two proverbs with me that enhanced my life. He used to apply proverbs as our parents did. He trained Livina in her secondary education with the help of Dada'm Cordelia.

Nigerian-Biafran Civil War 1967-1970 Red Cross: During the Nigerian Civil War, dede'm Sylvester secretly and bravely joined the Biafran army. He was trained as a Biafran soldier without the knowledge of our parents. As God would have it, he was rejected because of his height. Still eager to serve his people, he joined the Red Cross Society and became one of the rescuers who went to the war front to treat the wounded soldiers, both Nigerian and Biafran. He resigned after two ugly experiences in intense war zones. Once the war ended on the 10th of January, 1970, Dede'm Ikechi secured a teaching appointment and continued his normal life. After teaching for one year, he decided to further his education.

Further Education: Dede'm, being a hardworking, courageous and determined young man, enrolled at Alvan Ikoku Federal College of Education, Owerri, from 1980 to 1983 and earned his National Certificate in Education (NCE). In the course of this academic enhancement, an opportunity arose for him and he was upgraded and promoted to teach in secondary schools. He maintained his teaching appointment for over twenty years and retired honourably in 2010. As a teacher, he held such posts as Game Master, Agriculture Master, Labour Master, School Treasurer and School Secretary. In the community, his contributions were vital and numerous. He also used to be our Village Secretary and the leader of his traditional dancing group called Ebebu Dance. He was a man of few words but very intelligent and a man of action.

Matrimony: After teaching for some years, he got married. He married a non-Catholic woman but converted her to Catholicism and they were married in the church. The Marist Brothers of the Schools administered their marriage instructions. A few years after wedding, his peaceful life started to drift. He suffered like the biblical prophet Jeremiah, and at one point he wished he had chosen Jeremiah as his baptismal name instead of Sylvester. As an Igboland adage goes, things happen to a person according to the name he or she bears. Dede'm used to be an honourable and happy man until he married. Confusion entered his life with his wife, Comfort Chika Orji. Dede'm had five children with her: three boys and two girls. The adage "behind a successful man is a good wife" was not true in his case. Rather, his marriage led to his suffering and accidental death. One thing is certain, according to William Shakespeare: "The evil that men do lives after them." However, I disagree with Shakespeare because I believe that the evil that men do lives with them as it is already living with her and those of her contemporaries, both visible and invisible, who planned the evil act with her. The fight is God's (Exodus 14:14): "The Lord will fight for you; you need only to be still." In the book of Chronicles (20:1-29), it is said, "the battle is not yours, but God's..." Ikechi became a fallen Christian as a result of his dysfunctional marriage. Dede'm Ikechi, Ofojiogu, Ikejiofor, Sylvester Konye, Oganankpa, VC10. A talented, gentle teacher, a handsome man of integrity – rest in peace.

In 1967, with our younger brother, John Bosco.

Family Responsibility: Dede'm worked hard raising his five children. He sent his first son, Chisom, to Okporo Technical Secondary School and he passed with flying colours. Dede'm was willing to send any of his children to school to any level of education they wanted. He sent his son to Oko Polytechnic for more advanced academic education, but unfortunately he joined a cult and dropped out. Dede'm Ikechi picked up his courage and continued to educate his remaining four children. His second child was studying nursing at Imo State University and the others were in secondary school at the time of his sudden death.

Like our parents, he was a very industrious young man. He improved his house by building a big tank for drinking water and a big wall and other small rooms in the backyard for his children. He bought a car, and the children had bicycles. He was among the first men in the village to provide electricity for their families. We will never forget your tragic death on Tuesday, the 5th of April, 2011, at 10:00 in the morning. Though you are dead, your famous name liveth – rest in peace, VC10!

Odaaku Clementina (nee Konye Nwadike)

As the first daughter and the second child of the family, we addressed her Adanne-anyi and Dada-anyi, showing the respect due to our elders. Adanne-anyi Odaaku was born in 1948. Her name Odaaku means wealth. When she was born, according to our mother's narrative, she received a lot of gifts from people, and through her, many good things came to our parents. Dada'm Odaaku was the second mother we had when our mother was away. She was a role model to us. She lived an exemplary life, which all of us mirrored. She was a hardworking woman like our parents. She was a gentle, peaceful and persevering lady. As she was the first daughter of the family, we copied everything she did. If she had been bad, all of us would have been affected. Dada'm was a rare gem. Although our parents were practising traditional religion, they allowed all their children to practise the Christian religion. Dada'm Odaaku received her baptism and took the name Clementina. She was baptised as an adult, like our brother Ikechi. She completed primary school at Holy Rosary School, Orlu, then decided to go into business instead of furthering her education. Our parents supported her in her choice.

Domestic Chores: Mama trained Dada'm Odaaku well in domestic work, and she, with our mother, taught us well, too.

Nigerian-Biafran War: Dede'm Clementina joined the Red Cross Brigade during the Nigerian Civil War (1967-70). She helped to take care of *kwashiorkor* children. She came to the rescue of our family during the war. She provided relief materials such as food and clothing. We never lacked during the Nigerian Civil War.

Trader at Orlu Main Market: Dede'm Clementina began to do business at Orlu Town main market. She dealt in bags of rice and beans. She helped our parents to sustain the family until she got married.

Marriage: Dede'm Clementina was intended to marry the first child of Mr. Agu of Umueri village, Orlu. He went to fight in the Nigerian-Biafran War but never returned. She assumed that her proposed husband had gone into exile with Ojukwu Biafra, but when Ojukwu came back from Ivory Coast in 1980 without any soldiers, it dawned on her that she was hoping against hope. Adanne'm could not be consoled and refused to marry for years. Eventually, she married into the family of Fidelis Alisigwe, and they were wed at Holy Trinity Church, Orlu. Unfortunately, she did not give birth to any children because she was a little advanced in age and had endured such trauma. Adanne-anyi grieved deeply about not having any issue because she lived a chaste life. She was a woman of self-control and dignity. Her husband loved her very much, and they lived happily until she became ill and passed on. Ada, rest in peace.

Onyemachi

Onyemachi means "No one Knows Tomorrow." Our little brother, Onyemachi, was born in 1950. He was the third child of the family and the second son of my parents. He died quite young, as a teenager. Mama told me that he was a unique child; he was very smart in everything, and at one point, she started imagining what kind of being he might be. One couldn't whisper behind him. Before you thought about something, he would tell you what it was. Mama nicknamed him a **prophet**. She said that whatever he said then occurred, exactly. It was after his sudden death that Mama realized that God had sent him for a purpose. Onyii, rest in peace. That gift of prophecy in you never vanished among us. I inherited a little of it, and others have traces of it still. Some of us often see ahead of time future happenstances.

Ngamaeme Jeanefrances (nee Konye Nwadike)

According to our Igbo tradition, Dada'm Jane is popularly known as Ngamaeme, meaning "If I do not know how to do it, show me." Dada'm Ngamaeme was the fourth child and second daughter of our parents. She was born in 1952. As a result of deaths, she is now the first daughter of the family and by right accedes to the position of Adanneya. Adanne-anyi means the first daughter of the family. Dada'm Ngamaeme was baptised in the Catholic Church like her siblings, even though our parents were still non-Christian then. She was given the name Jeanefrances at baptism.

Marriage: She married into the family of Mr. Dim Osuala Leonard Senior. She was wed in the Catholic Church in Amike village. Her first son became the first priest among our grandchildren. Dada'm Jane, as all of her junior siblings call her, is quiet and gentle of heart. Like her parents, she hates injustice and is always fearless to speak out. Dada'm is a full-time housewife and she raised her ten children well. She has, presently, seven surviving boys and a girl. She is living a fulfilled married life with her husband and family. By the grace of God, she educated her children to university level. Three of her children studied at Imo State University. One studied at the Seat of Wisdom Seminary, the Washington Theological Union and the Diocese of Orlando Seminary, Florida, where he was ordained a Priest of God. One is a graduate of the Federal University of Technology, Owerri (FUTO) and read Computer Engineering in Lagos, Nigeria and is now a civil worker in the USA. One of her sons was a business manager in Jos Plateau State in the northern part of Nigeria. Another has a degree in Statistics from Benue State University, Nigeria. The rest are doing well in business.

Anyajiwe Henrietta (nee Konye Nwadike)

Dede'm Anyajiwe is the fifth child of our parents. She was born in 1954. Anyajiwe means jealous. As I've mentioned before, our parents gave their children their names based on the circumstances surrounding the child's birth. Dada'm Anyajiwe was very beautiful and was like a white baby when she was born. People admired her so much that our parents named her Anyajiwe. She attended primary school at Holy Rosary School, Orlu. After primary school, she decided to acquire sewing skills. She graduated and sewed clothes for several years until she had children.

Marriage: Dada'm Anyajiwe is married to Mr. Odikanwa Nwosu Declan of Umuna in our maternal homeland. She was wed in St. Joseph's Catholic Church, Umuna. She gave birth to seven children, four boys and three girls. They are all doing well in their different walks of life. Her first son, after his secondary education, left home for Lagos when it was the Nigerian business capital. Today, he is a business manager with boys serving as his apprentices. He gives them job opportunities. One daughter is a registered nurse in Spain, living happily with her husband and three children. Her other two daughters are graduates of Imo State University. Her first daughter is a graduate of Alvan Ikoku College of Education. One son is in Australia with his family, and another son is living and working in Thailand with his family. Dada'm Henrietta is a hard worker, like our parents. She is a market woman in Orlu Main Market. She sells pap and condiments at the market. Dada'm Henrietta has a compassionate, motherly heart. She loves to share what she has, no matter how little it is. She is a very prayerful lady with a devout faith. She is a very truthful lady and fearless in speaking out where there is injustice or unfairness. She doesn't mind the consequences of being truthful; she is a rare gem. Dada'm Anyajiwe is a hero and an outstanding member of our family. Dada'm, more power to your elbows.

Agwunihu Cordelia (nee Konye)

Dada'm Agwunihu is the sixth child of our parents. She was born on the 4th of March, 1956. She is my immediate senior. Our parents used to call her Agwunihu because of their ugly experiences with neighbours who, in their hearts, had ill feelings towards you but pretended to be friendly with you.

Schooling: She started her primary school at Holy Rosary School, Umuna Orlu, now Community School, Umuna Orlu, and finished up at Holy Trinity, Isigwu Umuna Udi. As our aunt, Lady Theresa Agu (nee Agim) got married, the Civil War stopped and her husband was transferred to Ezeagu County Grammar School, Udi. She followed them there, and after about two years, our brother-in-law was transferred back to Isu, his home town, so she started and completed her secondary school at Isu High School. After her secondary education, she started her auxiliary teaching, which lasted for nine months. With the money she'd earned, she paid for her training at Umudi Teacher Training College. While she was studying, our brother, Ikechi, also took to coaching her. She finished on the 1st of July, 1979, and was posted to a primary school. She assisted our elder brother in the training of two of her immediate younger sisters, one up to class five and one up to teachers' training college. Later, after her wedding, she furthered her education at Alvan Ikoku College of Education, Owerri. She completed her studies there in 1993. She taught in various schools such as Okwuabala Central School, Ihioma, Central Primary School, Amike, Central School, Okanazike, Central School, Eziachi, and Primary School, Umuzike, all in Orlu L.G.A. She paid for my education at Ihioma Girls Secondary School, Orlu. Dada'm, I appreciate your assistance. May the good Lord reward you abundantly! Remember, silver and gold have I none, but what I know for sure is that you are always in my prayers. I owe all of you, my siblings, my prayers. Anything I cannot do for you; God takes control of. He is the ultimate Master in charge.

Achievements: Dede'm Cordelia obtained the following certificates:

1. First School Leaving Certificate 1970
2. West African School Certificate 1976
3. Teacher's Grade Two Certificate 1979
4. Nigeria Certificate in Education 1993

Dada'm Agwunihu finally retired on the 1st of July, 2014. To God be the glory!

Marriage: On the 10th of August, 1985, she married her beloved husband, Mr. Christopher Oguadimma Nwosu, of Abor Eluama, Owerre-Ebeiri, in Orlu L.G.A. They were wed in Potiskum, Yobe State. Shown below is her wedding picture with our elder brother, the late Ikechi Konye, witnessing the ceremony. This made our family proud.

Dede'm Ikechi witnessing Dada'm Cordelia's wedding ceremony.

Her husband has been a businessman at Potiskuam for years. The marriage was blessed with five children, two girls and three boys, as follows: Ijeoma Juliet, Ikechukwu Benedict, Chinaemerem Irene, Eberechukwu Joachim, and Oluchukwu Michael. Thus far, Dada'm Cordelia has been blessed with seven grandchildren. Ijeoma Juliet gave birth to Cynthia Chine nye Alagwu, Gloria Chidimma Alagwu, Victor Chijoke Alagwu and Olivia Chidigo Alagwu. Chinaemerem Irene gave birth to Master Robert Nwachukwu Okoroji, Master Cyril Mary Chinwemeri Okoroji and Stella Marias Amarachukwu Okoroji. Dede'm Cordelia is following in the footsteps of my parents. Right from birth, they taught us the Christian way of life. Dede'm belongs to the Christian Women's Organization (CWO), Church Group 4, an Apostleship of Prayer and the League of the Sacred Heart. She is also a member of the Parish Council. In her lifetime, she has held many offices, such as secretary, treasurer, financial secretary, games mistress, labour mistress, regulator, sanitarian, general, disciplinarian and assistant headmistress.

Rose Ann Nkechinyerem
(Rev. Sr. Chinedum Joachim Konye Nwadike)

According to the genealogy of our family, I am the seventh of our parents' offspring. I was born on the 18th of April, 1958. At my birth, my parents gave me the name Nkechinyerem, which means "What God has given to me." In other words, the "Gift of God." At baptism, I was given the name Rose Ann. I was born in a pagan and non-academic family. Even though our family originally followed traditional religion, my siblings and I found our roots in the Christian religion. My parents introduced me to the Catholic Church and brought me up as a Christian child. Our mother called me Nne because she believed that I was the reincarnation of her grandmother.

Our paternal mother called me Nwamgbeke because I was born on Eke market day. In Igboland culture, Eke market day is viewed as a sacred day. For this reason, she always called me a blessed child. These traditional names given to me played a significant role in my life. They are the source of what I am today. Our elders say that people's names have an effect on them. Our mother and my siblings nicknamed me **Azuanuka, Tarzan, Ifesinachiabia and Nwadi Brothers.** During my religious profession, I took a new name, Chinedum, meaning, "**God leads Me" or "The Lord is my Shepherd.**" There was a huge change in my life after I chose this name. Our mother, when I chose this name, affirmed it and said to me, "Nne'm Rosa, *Nkechinyerem Nwa'm, Chineke gi ga edu gi na ije g*i." (Everything is happening according to her wish and blessings for me.) At this point, I am going to analyse the stages at which I achieved each goal, according to Erikson's theory of development. Human beings have been trying to imagine how things work and how the world came to be since they began to think. They kept gazing at the night sky full of stars and kept thinking about who put the stars there. They thought about father and mother, God the Creator, relationships, and the magic of interdependence in nature. They made models in the form of pictures of things they saw. They made models of their thinking about reality and spiritual self-discovery of self-awareness in relation to divine identity.

Here, I begin with my discussion of the normal development of the intellectual mind, self or personality and ego connected through self-awareness to the universal mind. Psychological development occurs in stages, which represent different age groupings. Some children may have fast or slow development within their age range according to their adaption to the environment through the use of reflexes or clues which they designate to represent the world. The adaptation to the environment is a continual process that leads to the assimilation and accommodation of facts into memory. These processes are used in life as the mind increasingly adapts to complex situations in the environment. Development is cumulative as certain learnings are achieved most effectively in certain periods of life according to the time of brain maturation. Psychological development can go backward as well as forward and can go by leaps and spurts. I will present the mental stage first each time as it tends to set the tone for learning and mental readiness. I will also specify each development stage with reference to what I was and what I did growing up.

Profile 1: Infancy (birth - 2 years): By trial and error, the baby explores the environment and establishes senses as the main doors through which information about the world is admitted. By the end of this period, a child has become a person. Our mother told me that when I was two years old, I used to be active and too sensitive. When I was hungry, wet, sleepy and alone, I would cry out for help. Mama told me that I was a serious and focused child and tried to explore everything. Papa made me a play-pen (ogbakwere) so I could move around safely.

Profile 2: Preschool (2 - 4 years): During this period, children develop their imaginations, the ability to use internal images in thinking and information processing. There is, however, rudimentary sorting and grouping which are the forerunners of later concept-formation. Near the end of this period, children may begin to have nightmares – an indication that imagination is fully developed. Identification proceeds here as children try to find out what kinds of people they are, and a question about how we feel about ourselves arises here, whether we have a sense of worthiness or competence. The developmental outcome of this period, according to Erikson, is autonomy vs shame and doubt. Self-regulation and self-control, as well as being able to control the impact of others on oneself or to say "No" to others, are important here. Self-awareness: at this stage, I knew that I was a girl. I was fond of saying, "My name is Rosy." When I was four, my first word was "mba", that is, no. According to my mother, I used to be a quiet and shy child. Whenever someone approached me, I would move backwards away from the person. Then I would turn and run to her. I loved to stay alone and explore things. She said I loved touching everything around me and looking at things closely, especially Dede'm Ikechi's books.

When they tried to take them away from me, I would scream and cry bitterly. I loved to listen and pay attention to any little sound or word, especially when people were talking. Mama also said that I used to obey commands and understand sign language whenever she made eye contact with me. She told me that I loved any green material, so she once bought me a nice green gown. I am much the same today. I still love to hold and read books, and I still love green the most.

Profile 3: School Age (5 - 12 years): Here, the process of internalization begins. The self-critic is based upon all parental admonitions and prohibitions and what the individual carries, henceforth, within himself or herself as the standards for behaviour and moral values as taught by parents. From this point, intellectual development accelerates. Peer groups begin to take centre stage. Conformity learning begins, and the developmental task here is initiative vs guilt. Around age 7, the stage of concrete operations is brought in: learning to perform logical mental operations. Skills of all sorts emerge, and children discover some things they do well and focus attention on developing these in school. School age ushers in industry vs inferiority complex. If a child feels incompetent, inferiority feelings result, but if not, he or she learns how to work and develop new skills.

Life in the Village: When I was between the ages of five and twelve, I used to be strong-willed and determined. If I had something to do, I become focused till I achieve the goal. I used to gather firewood, a tin pot, water and vegetables and begin to cook, imitating my mother. I used to sit in front of our kitchen door, watching my mother cooking. Sometimes, my mates and I played mothers, going to market to sell and purchase food items, cooking, going to farm, or visiting our friends for condolences. We would go to one end of the bush and begin to talk, saying, "Oh sorry, we learnt that somebody died." And we would pretend to be crying. Sometimes, we carried little toy babies on our backs as if they were real babies. When we felt they were hungry, we fed them and let them sleep, just as our mothers used to do for us. When I was growing up in our noble village, Ndiowerre-Orlu, we loved one another, did things together, had peer-group farming (oru mbiri) and young girls had meetings on Sundays (ibu-otu umu agboghi obea). These meetings were rotated, and our parents, especially our mothers, supported us by buying food items for the meetings. Our mothers would cook a tray of rice with goat meat and prepare "ibibe" (tapioca – sliced cassava with vegetable sauce) and oil-bean food for us to serve to our age mates. On those occasions, we were all happier than usual. We had a sense of sharing and forbearing. Our mothers were always on our side to support, guide and be role models to us. We used to fetch fire from each other's houses, ate together, shared vegetables and crops together, moved freely together, fetched water from the streams and taps together, fetched firewood from the bushes, borrowed things from our neighbours, and went out in the night together to pick up snails from the bushes during the first rains of the year. We also used to go out together to pick African star apples (udara) and mangos in our village square at night and very early in the mornings. Both boys and girls came out for moonlight play. It was a time when we called each other my sister and my brother (nwanne'm na nwanna'm) from the bottom of our hearts and meant it. It was a time when individuals were happy about the progress and achievement of others. I used to go alone down the hill behind the Bishop Shanahan College (BSC) and former Bishop Shanahan Training College, Orlu, to harvest cassava, wash ibibe (tapioca) in the stream, fetch firewood, farm and collect breadfruit for my mother when the land was at peace with our ancestors, and nothing happened to me but now reverse is the case.

Nigerian-Biafran Civil War: A Big Hindrance to My Education

There was a big interval before I was enrolled in primary school. This was as a result of the Nigerian-Biafran Civil War from 1967 to 1970, and it set me back academically. However, I survived it. I entered primary school at the age of twelve. I had absolutely nothing academically in my head. My head was like John Locke's concept of the child's mind – a blank slate or tabula rasa - as far as academics were concerned. I kept on struggling, trying to catch up. At school, I would remember only the poems and lessons sung as songs. The rest of the lectures would remain absent from my brain. I always felt bad. All this time, I had low self-esteem. I always withdrew and would try to think of ways to help my situation. In the classroom, I maintained average results. The most important thing is that I always worked strenuously to improve myself until I succeeded in doing so. Our mother would come to me and say, "Nne'mu' Rosa, what is the matter? Come out and brighten your face." Then she would send me on an errand to distract me. This is where she was an expert in applying her natural counselling skills.

I started primary school at Holy Rosary School, Orlu, and later transferred to Practicing School 1, Orlu. When I finished class four, I transferred to Premier Primary School, Amike, where I finished my primary education and obtained my First Leaving Certificate. One thing was obvious: I loved going to school, and Papa and Mama were good motivators of education. They would always make sure that all their children attended school, come rain or shine. Our father never liked to hear that we'd been sent home from school for not paying school fees. He would say, "Take the money and go back to your school and read." Livy, my young sister, and I would plan to stay at home to play, but Papa would never let us stay behind. At school, I loved Physical Exercise (PE), so Papa bought green uniforms for my immediate younger sister and me. This is where I developed my interest in green as my natural colour. Anywhere I see the colour green, I fall in love with it. My teachers loved to make me the leader of their farm team. Each farming season, they would select me to lead their farm workgroups to direct the students in what to do. On the completion of my primary school education, I engaged in petty trading, selling peanuts and moi-moi (steamed bean pudding), made pomade from palm oil, and helped my parents with farming and household chores.

Profile 4: Adolescence (12 - 18 years): Adolescence is a bridge between childhood and adulthood and provides a long period during which young people can learn the skills required in a complex industrial society. Intellectual development reaches maturity, and a person can now think about his or her thinking – introspect. Physical maturity leads to an interest in the opposite sex. Peer influences reach their peak, and parental advice is likely rejected in a primary bid for independence. The female sex-role model is now enforced by everyone because of human vulnerability to mistakes. Ego identity, as defined by Erikson (1968), is the perception of a central self, and this perception needs to be matched by validating feedback from others that they see one in the same way. I was very lucky in adolescence; my mother helped me a lot through her advice. She emphasised the need for a young girl to keep herself pure to avoid problems. At this age, I worked as a maid. I was a housemaid for some years because I was so loyal that each time our parents asked me to go and work for someone, I would go. This helped me to be responsible and very adaptive to any kind of environment I find myself in. It also assisted me in building a good relationship between my family and the families I worked for.

Profile 5: Young Adulthood (18 - 21 years): This is an era of emancipation. Persons of this age group usually leave home, and attending a status college is an option for many, while others go to work and become financially independent. If encouraged, thinking may develop to a reasonable conclusion, and creativity, if it survived schooling, may blossom and bear fruit. It is a prime time of life because skills and energy are optimal and hope is high.

I gained admission to Ihioma Girls' Secondary School, Orlu, in 1978. This school was formerly called Holy Rosary School, Ihioma, Orlu (HOROSCO). During our common entrance exam, I wished for Ihioma Girls, and it manifested. I desired it because I'd heard about the reputation of the school. When I enrolled, I thought it was a convent school, but it wasn't. However, it had every discipline of the convent ethos. We received every moral discipline, vocational training and academic training, social and otherwise. We had Reverend Brother Nwokem from the Marist Brothers of the Schools as our Dean of Studies, Rev. Brother Joachim Ezetulugo, who came often to give moral instruction to the students, Rev. Fathers from Regina Pacis Parish, Ihioma, and the Rev. Sisters from Immaculate Heart Convent who were both our academic teachers and our moral instructors. I was class prefect of my various classes from Class One till Class Five. I received a Certificate of Best Behaved in my class.

Every student who studied there from the 1970s to the 1980s acquired a sound education and a moral foundation. This school produced a lot of reverend sisters. The most remarkable thing is that all my acquaintances at school are reverend sisters today. It gives me great joy and upliftment to look back. My academic years there were not in vain. I am still very grateful to our honourable principal, Mrs. Okonkwo, and the late Rev. Br. Nwokem of the Marist Brothers of the Schools ("our darling Brother" as the students used to address him), as well as Rev. Sr. Dominica Odita of the Immaculate Heart Sisters, who gave us effective discipline in that academic period. Ihioma Girls prepared me well for my religious vocation.

Among the subjects I studied there were English Language, Mathematics, Literature, Biology, Agricultural Science, History, Religious Knowledge, French, and Geography. At the end of secondary school, I failed some of my papers, so I began to prepare for the General Certificate Examination (GCE). I found myself at Secondary School, Dikenafai, in Ideato Local Government Area, Imo State, to complete my English and mathematics papers. Rev. Brother Andrew Iwuagwu of the Marist Brothers of the Schools, who was the principal there, offered my colleagues and me scholarships to pass our papers, yet we did not obtain the required mark. I always remembered my mother's proverb that what makes a hen search for food in the rain is important to her. I emulated Abraham Lincoln when he was seeking to become the American president. He failed eleven times before he succeeded. I eventually succeeded academically and became what I am today. God's timing is the best.

> *"I get knocked down but I get up again and you'll never keep me down."*
> - Chumbawamba (Tubthumping)

> *"I'm thankful for my struggle because without it I wouldn't have stumbled across my strength."*
> - Alex Elle

> *"Get up, dress up, show up, and never give up."*
> - Genevieve Rhode

> *"I don't know where I'm going, but I'm on my way."*
> - Carl Sagan

While still in quest of academic success, I became involved in church activities. My life was spent in the church, and there was nothing anyone could do to convince me to change. I was really crazy about church activities then. I taught children and adult catechism, and I was in the Block Rosary. I remained obedient to my parents and did my domestic duties and church duties as well. I was even prepared to die for the church; my zeal was so high and I was rooted in spiritual activities. I travelled far and wide for Block Rosary crusades with the late Mr. and Mrs. Ben Ibenachu of Akata na Nnempi of Orlu Local Government Area. This family was one of my role models in spiritual adventure and enhancement. May they rest in p**eace** – Amen.

It was through the Block Rosary that I learned the story of the three Fatima Shepherds, Francisco, Jacinta and Lucia. In 2014, I was thrilled to visit Fatima before my Religious Silver Jubilee celebration. I toured around their home, entered their various rooms, visited their graves and their church where they were baptised and worshipped, and saw where they used to pasture their sheep and where our Blessed Mother Mary appeared to them. I took some pictures of their bedrooms and the articles they used. I brought this picture home to encourage you, my younger ones. Your prayers and your Block Rosary membership are not in vain; they hold great blessings for you in the future.

Fatima shepherds   My Fatima friends and I

The three little children are called the Fatima Shepherds: Francisco, Jacinta and Lucia. The three Sisters here with long habits are my friends with whom I stayed at Fatima. They took me around to see where these children lived before they passed on. My prayerful vigil group at Southend Victoria made this trip possible for me. May God reward you all immensely. My Block Rosary group and I always prayed at our village square at five o'clock every morning and six o'clock every evening. I was a member of the Mary League Girls and the Confraternity of Christian Doctrine (CCD). These activities enhanced my aspiration towards the religious life, with the blessing of our mother. Our parents were very supportive of the spiritual aspect of my growth. This enabled me to teach catechism for quite a long time at the Holy Trinity Church, Orlu, now the Holy Trinity Cathedral Parish. Many of my catechumens became reverend fathers and sisters. Rev. Fr. Sylvester Dunu and my nephew, Rev. Fr Leonard Dim, are among those I taught. I was also a member of the Society of St. Anthony of Padua where I was inspired to serve the poor and the needy and joined The Holy Family Sisters of The Needy Congregation in the service of the poor.

On my journey to religious life, I explored two congregations, namely, the Holy Child congregation and the congregation of Fr. Ede. One day, I met Rev. Brother Andrew Iwuagwu of the Marist Brothers of the Schools and asked him to introduce me to a convent where I could become a reverend sister. He gave me the name of Rev. Sr. Rose Uchenna Nwosu and her convent address at Calabar. One day after morning mass, I asked Mary Unugo, now Rev. Sr. Mary Amauche Unugo, to go with me to Calabar to visit Rev. Sister Rose Nwosu, and she asked me to inform her father. When I informed him, he agreed and said to me, "Go with your sister. I know you will not mislead her." So, one afternoon, the two of us set out for Calabar. When we arrived, Sr. Unchenna asked us our names, and I introduced myself as Rose Ann and my colleague introduced herself as Mary Amauche. Sr. Nwosu pretended to beat us up for adding something to our names instead of leaving them exactly like hers. She really welcomed us warmly and made a lasting impression on us. She gave us a thorough introduction to their way of life and their congregation; at the end, she asked us to go home to reflect and get back to her. She was eager to see the two of us back.

For over a year, I kept praying about it, but my mind was still focused on serving the poor and the needy. When I told Mary about it, she disclosed that she was interested in the Holy Child Sisters, and I encouraged her to proceed. Another person I encountered when I was seeking a congregation to join was Rev. Sr. Ambrose Oforegbu, then Miss Perpetual Oforegbu, who introduced me to Fr. Emmanuel Ede's congregation. I went there to just spend one night. I saw that God was not calling me there, thus, at Mass in the morning, during consecration, I asked God not to grant me the favour of visiting there. However, Father interviewed me and wanted me to come back with Sr. Ambrose, who was in the village for a short visit. He asked me to bring my things along with me for live in, but when I reached home, I dodged Sr. Ambrose till she left for the convent.

After that, I had to inform my spiritual directors – the Marist Brothers – about it and what I really wanted. Eventually, I met with The Holy Family Sisters of the Needy during one of the celebrations at Orlu Cathedral by His Lordship Rt. Rev. Dr. Gregory O. Ochiagha, Bishop Emeritus of Orlu Diocese, and inquired about them. I then met Rev. Brother Andrew Iwuagwu, who took me to St. Paul's, Owerri, to meet the founder of The Holy Family Sisters of the Needy, the Very Rev. Dennis Mary Joseph Ononuju C.S.Sp, who carefully explained to me the charism of his foundation, their goal and what they do to help the poor and the needy. While he was talking, I kept on saying in my mind, *this is my congregation*. And behold, when Brother and I came out to proceed home, he said to me, "My child, as long as I have known you, this has been your way of life. What do you think?" And I responded to him saying, "Brother, this is my congregation." So, it came to be the way the Holy Spirit had prompted me. When I reached home, I told our mother my experiences and what I thought. She then gave me the go-ahead and her blessing. Nevertheless, I was scared to inform my elder brother, Ikechi. But our mother encouraged me not to be afraid and promised to accompany me to tell Dede'm Ikechi. When we met Dede in his corridor, where he was sitting and relaxing, I unveiled my desire to him, expecting a "no" and a "why" from him. But the answer was, "If you know that you can make it, go ahead. I wish you good luck." I was overwhelmed with joy, and our mother was, too.

In our village, I used to be the leader of my dancing group. I danced like my mother, and I used proverbs a lot when speaking, like my mother too. As I was brought up in a non-Christian family at the time, I grew to love the social life and good traditions of my people, through which I made the acquaintance of my traditional ruler, the late Eze Patrick Achonoun, Ezeigwe of Orlu, who influenced and promoted the culture of our people. The relationship with Igwe extended to his first daughter, Ada Veronica Igwe. I met her in London where we became friends, and we still are, to date.

In 1995, with the late Igwe, Eze Patrick Achononu, during my Final Commitment Reception at Holy Trinity Cathedral, Parish Orlu.

An Igboland proverb says, "If a child washes his hands well, he eats with the elders." This means that our elders respect the youth if they conduct themselves well. In Igboland, any child is a child for all. If a child does well, everybody in the village, and the town at large, appreciates his or her efforts and presence. If a child misbehaves or misrepresents the society, it affects everyone. Hillary Rodham Clinton used the African proverb "It Takes a Village To Raise A Child" as the title of her book.

The late Ezeigwe of Orlu had especial respect for me not because I am a religious but for being a hardworking young lady and a good citizen of Orlu. I used to visit him in his palace. He often offered me kola nuts to pray over before we ate them; he would then chat and tell me of the happenings around our town. I was glad to see him in his ripe old age. I visited him in 2001 and ate kola nuts with him and my nephew, Onyemaucheckwu Dim. That was my last visit before he passed on into eternity in 2003. I am not telling this short story to be praised but to motivate the young to dwell on doing the right things so they will also inherit the blessings of the elders. Seeing myself standing at Nnanyi Igwe's side gives me joy, though with mixed feelings now that he is no more. May he rest in peace – Amen.

> *"You become like the people you spend the most time with."*
>
> - Jack Canfield
> The Success Principles

Referring to the above quotation, I am advising you, the younger generation, to hang around with those who would influence your life positively. It pays enormously to be among positive role models – they are a treasure. I have reached where I am at this moment because I followed in the footprints of my parents, siblings and good people around me. I have been average in all aspects, but copycatting outstanding individuals has helped me upgrade myself in all directions. Do the same and stop hanging around with good-for-nothing fellows. Jack Canfield advises you and me to do the following: ***"Drop out of the "AIN'T it awful" club ... and surround yourself with successful people"*** (p.189). To reinforce this statement, just read the advice below very attentively:

> *"There are two types of people – anchors and motors. You want to lose the anchors and get with the motors because the motors are going somewhere and they're having fun. The anchor will just drag you down."*
>
> - Wyland
World-renowned artist

At this juncture, I would love you to judge for yourself which people you would love to follow: the "anchors" or the "motors"? As you make your bed, so you lie on it. Follow the motors and be your authentic self.

In 1983, after my secondary education, I made a list of things I planned to achieve while waiting for God's will for me. One of my priorities on the list was acquiring typing skills. The other items on the list were to plant a tomato garden, acquire basic nursing skills, attend driving school, and go to a convent. On a Monday morning, I walked down to Orlu main town to meet a woman typist with whom I'd lived in her father's compound when I was in secondary school at Ihioma Girls; that was the Ojimba family at Ihioma. I disclosed my reason for seeking her out, and she was happy to assist me. She charged me the sum of five Naira (N5.00) weekly for training me in typing. I was very excited to master it. I immediately started out as a typist and became self-employed at Orlu Town. This gave me an opportunity to think about what I really wanted to do next. My lifetime ambition has been to uplift myself in my career and to assist others to improve themselves. While thinking about what next to do, another opportunity emerged with the help of the Marist Brothers of the Schools. The Brothers introduced me to Nnaji and Sons Printing Press, Orlu, where I was first employed as a typist and then as a receptionist. I quit my self-employed job and secured the job there. I used the first money I earned to purchase a wrapper for our mother in appreciation of her being a good mother and a role model to me and my siblings. I continued doing this job and the gardening as a hobby. Then I motivated my younger sister, Chigoziri Christiana, to learn the same skill. I paid for her to learn it, and she acquired the skill successfully.

In 1986, I had a call to religious life, and I left home for the convent and abandoned everything else. After an Aspirancy period of a few months, I was received into Postulancy on the 21st of February, 1987. At the completion of my six-month postulancy training, I was clothed as a Novitiate on the 10th of November, 1988. One December season, our mother sent

Dada'm Henrietta Odikanwa and my kinsman, Mr. Anthony Madueke, to visit me and inform me that she had started attending the Catholic Church. My joy became complete. Mama witnessed my First Profession on the 22nd of August, 1990, and my Final Commitment on the 2nd of September, 1995, at Assumpta Cathedral, Owerri.

In 1995. Mama and Dede'm Ikechi (in yellow tunic) witnessing my Final Commitment in Assumpta Cathedral, Owerri. Behind them are my Orlu indigenous reverend sisters.

Mama and Dede'm Ikechi – rest in peace. I am glad Mama died and was buried as a Christian, which was my ultimate goal. Our present Bishop, Bishop Augustine T. Ukwuoma, gave her the final blessing before she was laid to rest. This is one of the reasons for the joy and pride of our family.

Towards the completion of the Novitiate, I went for apostolic work at Umulowo Hospital where I worked as a receptionist, data collector and issuer of cards for incoming patients to see their doctor. At the end of the apostolic work, I made my First Religious Commitment in 1990 and took a new name, Reverend Sister Chinedum Joachim, and gave up Nkechinyerem Rose Ann.

Profile 6: Adulthood (22 - 40 years): The task for adults, according to Erikson, is generativity vs stagnation or success vs failure. Generativity means taking responsibility for society. Marriage may occur and parenting begins; a home is created and love and work are two main aspects of life. If the spiritual reawakening is begun now, the heart may reopen and enable the person to create deeper, more satisfying relationships.

On the 15th of February, 1991, I found my feet on the soil of the United States of America. I had been sent for missionary work and to study. I landed at New York City Airport and then flew to Washington DC National Airport. My religious sister, who travelled with me, and I stayed with our religious sisters in Washington DC for a few months and then relocated to Pennsylvania to work with vulnerable young mothers. Later, we were recalled to enrol at the University of District of Columbia, Washington DC. We finished one academic year and were asked to proceed to the University of Villanova, Pennsylvania, where we enrolled in a nursing course. We finished one semester with a partial scholarship, and we did well on the course. As a result of inadequate arrangements for accommodation, we were ordered to move to Scranton, Pennsylvania, so that one of us might secure admission to Scranton University. We then requested our transcripts and sent them to the unknown university. We moved into Scranton, but the Sister who had invited us there had no place for us to stay. We hung on till the Rev Sister M. Gabriel Kane, I.H.M. in charge of Women Religious in Pennsylvania came to our rescue and gave us a place to rest our heads.

We acted in obedience and enrolled at Lackawanna Junior College Pennsylvania for Medical Secretarial study for two years. From university, we found ourselves in a junior college. However, the school granted us a loan to enable us to continue our studies. After completion of the course, we graduated and received an Associate Degree in Medical Secretarial Diploma (ADMS) with honours. At this point, we took different directions. I met with financial difficulties and other ups and downs, and disappointment set in. But instead of losing hope, I fortified myself and kept rolling on towards the attainment of my career objective. Working harder and seeking solutions became the goal of the day. I was lucky enough to secure a part-time job at North Eastern Plastic Industry, Scranton, Pennsylvania, and also secured admission to Penn State University, Pennsylvania. I combined the work with my studies. While doing that, I was recalled by my congregation to move over to Washington DC, so I abandoned everything and proceeded. When I reached Washington DC, I was readmitted to the University of the District of Columbia. Things did not work out well there as a result of financial constraints. I left there for Strayer University, Washington DC, where they granted me the opportunity needed; there I completed both my Bachelor of Science degree in Computer Information Systems (BSCIS) and a Master of Science degree in Business Administration (MSBS). The Sisters of the Immaculate Heart Convent, Scranton, Pennsylvania, allowed me to continue residing in their convent while working and attending school. I sought admission to Penn State University, but the Dean of Studies refused to admit me when he went through my documents and saw how I had transferred from one school to another within a short period.

I explained to him it was as a result of my religious status and that wherever the authority asked me to go I had to obey. Luckily for me, I went there with the Superior General of the Immaculate Heart Sisters, who reinforced my explanations. He accepted these and gave me admission. Precisely what he was afraid of reoccurred. After one academic year, I was asked to go back to Washington DC to manage our house there. I packed up everything and went. In Washington, I vowed not to practise blind obedience anymore because it was causing me psychological trauma. Consequently, I put a full stop to unnecessary movement. I strove hard and combined my daily tasks with my religious activities. I secured a menial job to pay my academic debts, but it was so difficult. I was fortified by this quote:

> *"You must see positive possibilities in the midst of the storm no matter how bad it might seem!"*
> - Margaret Dureke
> Words And Phrases Of Wisdom For Spiritual
> and Emotional Upliftment 2002 (p. 51)

I firmly believed that God had called me into religious life; otherwise, I would have called it quits at this point, but the Good Shepherd led me through; I kept on rolling with hope and faith.

> *"Blessed be God, who neither ignored my prayer nor deprived me of his love." (Psalm 66:20)*
> The Jerusalem Bible, Popular Edition Darton,
> London & Todd 1974, (p. 732).

If anything is fruitful, you never quit; no matter how difficult it is, keep trying your best till you succeed. Quitters are the losers. Never be a loser. "We prove ourselves by great fortitude in times of suffering, in times of hardship and distress" (2 Cor. 6:4-5). In any difficult situation, remember that endurance is mighty power and patience gives many good things. With endurance, you will achieve a lot. However, according to Dureke, do the following:

> ***Cry if you will, complain if you will, shout if you will but you must never quit. Quitters are losers! PERIOD! No matter how many times you tried before, don't ever give up. Just keep on keeping on even if you die trying. The only way you will not succeed is if you quit.***
>
> - Margaret Dureke
> Words and Phrases of Wisdom from Spiritual and Emotional Upliftment 2002 (p. 16).

I secured a job at the Nursing Biology Library at the Catholic University of America in Washington DC, entering data, organizing books, lending, and recording information. Below are various pictures taken when I was working there. I never knew that I would write a book on the Pride of the Konye Family. Only God inspired me to write this book, and

I used this opportunity to retrieve all my past memories as I write along. This is why I always believe that with God all things are possible, and with the ministry of possibilities, one can always conquer impossibilities.

In 1996, working in the Nursing Biology Library of the Catholic University of America.

On the completion of my MSBA, I proceeded to do a PhD in Psychology at Lacrosse University, Louisiana, and obtained it summa cum laude. I also gained State of Maryland Board of Nursing Assistant Certification and District of Columbia Nursing Assistant Certification from the University of the District of Columbia, Washington DC, that enabled me to work with elderly people at Providence Hospital, Washington DC branch of Carroll Manor, and Christ Kingdom Group Home. I also worked with the Institute of Psychotherapy with children with non-compliant behaviour.

I have associated with many people from all walks of life with various experiences.

In the USA, I combined spiritual life with assiduous work despite all odds. I helped the Igbo Catholics in the Archdiocese of Washington DC. I was the Assistant Coordinator of the Children Igbo Catechism. I was the Liturgy Directress and Directress of adult and children Igbo Lectors' Association. I was also the Spiritual Directress of the Igbo Catholic Women Association of Blessed Tansi. For my commitment and hard work with the Nigerian Igbo faithful, I was awarded an inscribed plaque.

The picture below is of me driving to work. I am very grateful to Rev. Sr. Helen Scarry, R.J.M. (former Secretary for Service of Women Religious Washing DC.), who donated this car to me. May God reward you immensely. The car, a Ford Escort AF5516, was donated when I had no driving skills, and I had to learn to drive. It is only courageous individuals that can take on the challenge of driving in a foreign land! "I can do all things through Christ who strengthens me" (Philippians 4:13). I drove the car from 1997 to 2008, to church, to work and to the market, and it made my life a lot easier. I am not showing off but encouraging you, the younger generation, to take on challenges; without challenges, one cannot succeed in life. Do not be afraid – you can do it.

Eventually, as a result of my ardent efforts, I became a citizen of the United States of America. During the process of obtaining my citizenship certificate, I was called to have my fingerprints taken and didn't know that I would be asked to take the US History Test the same day. I took it and scored 100% – God is great! With my American passport, I was privileged to travel to the United Kingdom as a missionary when asked by my Superior General. I arrived in the UK on the 31st of May, 2008.

Profile 7: Middle Age (40 - 55 years): This period is marked by adaptation, whether successful or unsuccessful in one's vocation. There may be a surge of discontent leading to a mid-life crisis such as neurosis, divorce, addiction or vocational change. I am happy at this age; I am fulfilled in what I have achieved. I am still a nun. I have worked in different fields with different types of people. I have had a great impact on the lives of many. I did my missionary work in both the USA and the UK. I wrote two books, *Building Up Self-Confidence – A Fundamental Way of Conquering Fear* and *Ancestral Legacy of Family Counselling,* the latter is now on the global market.

Profile 8: Aging (55 years): This era has its own unique challenges. Retirement coupled with physical slowing down means people may re-evaluate their priorities. Endurance usually declines, and illness and disability may appear. The crisis here is integrity (wholeness) vs despair. How does one maintain a sense of wholeness throughout all the changes that are taking place? A return to spiritual activities at this time may be welcome. At this age, I am still working hard to help children in their breakfast club and after-school club. I was a registered counsellor with the Association of Christian Counsellors to help women in pregnancy crises. I used to be first chairperson of the Holy Family Sisters of the Needy Charity Trust in London. I celebrated my silver jubilee anniversary (25 Years) of my religious life in the Congregation of the Holy Family Sisters of the Needy and remain a full-fledged member. I am fulfilled as a human being, and I am happy for what I could achieve. I feel actualized.

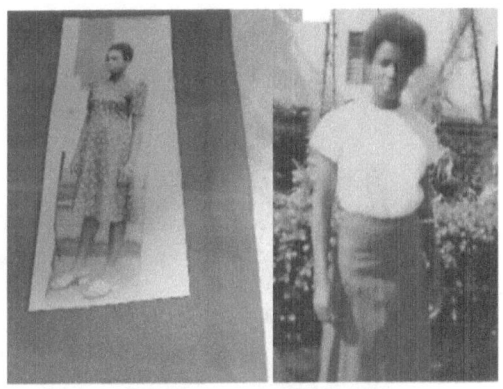

In 1986. First Stage – Aspirancy towards religious attainment.

In 1986. Second Stage – Postulancy.

In 1989. Third Stage – Novitiate.

22nd August 1990. Fourth Stage – about to do First Religious Profession, robed in wedding gown.

22nd August 1990. Fourth Stage – First Religious Profession, clothed in full habit.

2nd September 1995. Final Stage: Final Commitment – friends celebrating with me.

The last picture was taken on my final commitment with friends celebrating with me. I am the one in the blue robe. These are priests, a reverend brother and my fellow reverend sisters sharing my joy. This is the ultimate pride of the Konye Family. I am blessed because two unique individuals in this group photograph – Rev. Br. Joseph Muoka and Rev. Fr. Felix Elosi – are the architects of my spiritual life. Brother Muoka is the one with a cross hanging around his neck and a black cord around his waist, while Father Elosi is the one on the extreme right. These two Reverends taught and motivated me towards the way of God when I was one of their catechumens at the Holy Trinity Church, Orlu. During our confirmation period, Brother Muoka said to us, "Now that you are about to receive confirmation, you are qualified to go into the world to teach others." His words empowered me to join the Confraternity of the Christian Doctrine (CCD), and I began to teach catechism. I was able to produce some priests and reverend sisters from my class; you will read more details about this further on. Brother Muoka and Father Elosi are part of the joy and pride of my family. Thanks so much for your contribution to my spiritual life that led to what I am today. I can't narrate my history without mentioning you.

While working in the UK, I went to abortion clinics to pray with and counsel the girls who went in for abortions. I made friendly approaches to them and asked them to keep their babies instead of terminating them. I held monthly meetings and presented talks for vulnerable young mothers, educating them on the need for choosing life. I uplifted them and encouraged them to move on with their lives.

I also extended my spiritual activities to St. Pious X Catholic Church. I used to be a Liturgical Reader and a Spiritual Directress for the Legion of Mary – Our Lady of Good Counsel Presidium. As a devoted religious, I was always ready to help the faithful wherever needed. Likewise, I read in the Igbo Catholic Community Mass every second Sunday of the month.

22nd August 2015. Religious Silver Jubilee Anniversary Celebration.

In the UK, I was assigned the role of community Superior and the first Zonal Leader of The Holy Family Sisters of the Needy, English Zone, and Chair of the HFSN Board of Trustees for the HFSN Charity, UK. I believe in the "Mystery of Possibilities" that always leads me towards success. Beverley Randall believes that everyone should take the time to think about what they really want to do because, as she puts it,

> *"it is not where you start that matters but where you end up that counts."*
>
> - Beverley Randall
> Pride of Black British Women 1995 (p. 52)
> By Deborah King

In 2013. Missionary Activities in the United Kingdom. These are some of the babies saved from the abortuary.

Although my parents were non-Christians, I became the first Reverend in my village. An Igbo adage, *onye kwe chi ya kwe*, means if you agree, your God consents. So, do not sleep; awaken and work yourself up. I am an expert in time management. I used time well and this led to my huge success in life when I knew that age was covering me with its heavy blanket. I plead with you to plan your time properly in order to be successful, self-confident and self-actualized individuals.

> *"If you are positive and confident about yourself, nothing can stop you from achieving what you want in life."*
>
> - Maxine Chandler
> Pride of Black British Women 1995 (p. 30)
> By Deborah King

As I was writing, it occurred to me that I have a book on words of wisdom. I immediately laid hold of the book and came across the phrase below. I began to reflect on how I succeeded in reaching self-actualization. Yes, I strongly believe in self-empowerment, as Dureke puts it. Without it, one heads nowhere. I remember in primary and secondary school, I absolutely disempowered myself from learning mathematics; to this day, I have never had the ability or willingness to learn it. Hence, in one of my books titled, *Building Self-confidence*, I emphasize the role fear plays in people's lives. My main purpose in writing that book was to fight fear in myself and others. Believe me, I succeeded in winning the battle through self-empowerment, just as our parents did.

> *"The power of belief is the key to self-empowerment and self-empowerment is equal to success! Without self-empowerment it is impossible to believe in yourself and when you don't believe in yourself, you can't be empowered to achieve."*
>
> - Margaret Dureke
> Author & Motivational Speaker
> Words and Phrases of Wisdom for Spiritual
> and Emotional Upliftment 2002 (p. 1)

Here, I can testify that my parents, my siblings, and I believed in self-empowerment and we were able to reach where we are today. We never let our parents' light go out. Never give up on your dreams, no matter the situation. Have a positive belief in yourself because your belief, whether positive or negative, will have an effect on you. You can move mountains if you have positive belief. You can achieve your ultimate aspiration if you trust and believe in your will power. Remember, ability and willingness ignite you towards success. Whatever you achieve is what you have allowed yourself to achieve.

> *"Our beliefs can move us forward in life – or they can hold us back. Wherever you are in life, look at your beliefs. They put you there."*
>
> - Oprah Winfrey

O The Oprah Magazine
The Best of Oprah's What I Know for Sure
September 2000 (pp. 8-9)

"Children are like sponges, soaking up everything they are taught, directly and indirectly, as they develop into the hugely complex being an adult is. Babies learn astonishingly fast. Things we take for granted, such as walking and talking, are immensely complicated, requiring a learning curve steeper than anything you will ever encounter again. As an adult the new things you learn will be much simpler, indeed, you may go many months without learning anything new at all. "

- Sarah Litvinoff

Uloaku Ngozie Livina (nee Konye) (Mrs. Declan Onyeajuwu (Engr.)

Uloaku Ngozie Livina is my immediate younger sister. She was born on the 11th of April, 1960, in Ndiowerre Village, Orlu. Our parents named her Uloaku because everybody was expecting mama to give birth to a baby boy instead. When she gave birth to her, people said, "A girl again!" Then my parents named her Uloaku, which means "the house of wealth." Or "wealth has come." Ngozie and I grew up together and went to the same primary school, but we attended different secondary schools. When she grew up, she took another name, Ngozi, for reasons best known to her. She also was given a nickname which means "if the eye is a gun." This was because she always eyed people. At baptism, she was named Livina. Now she is known as Mrs. Livina Ngozi Onyeajuwa (nee Livina Ngozi Uloaku Konye Nwadike).

Marriage: In 1986 she married into the family of Mr. Engr. Declan Onyeajuwa at Eluama Umuowa in Orlu Local Government Area. She was wed in the Catholic Church. She has given birth to five children, all boys.

Educational Background: She obtained her first Leaving Certificate from Practicing School one, Orlu (1976/1977). She also earned her West African School Certificate from Ojike Memorial Secondary School in 1983. In 1986, Nne Livy, being as hard-working as our parents, enrolled in Bishop Shanahan Teachers' Training College, Umuna, where she attained her Teaching Grade II Certificate. She also gained admission to Osun State College of Education, Ilesha, Osun State, and obtained the National Certificate of Education in Guidance/ Counselling and Social Studies in 1993. Still striving to advance her education, she registered at Lagos State University, Ojo, for Guidance Counselling and Social Studies as a Teaching Subject in 2003.

Work Experience: Ngozie taught in the National Youth Service Corps, at Primary School, Osogbo, Osun State, in 1994 and at St. Leo's Nursery/Primary School, Oke Oniti, Osogbo, from 1994 to 2003. She extended her teaching experience to Amazing Grace Nursery/Primary/Secondary School, Osogbo, Osun State, from 2008 to 2011.

Position Held: President of the Catholic Students' Association of Nigeria at Bishop Shanahan Teachers' Training College, Umuna.

Games Captain of the school.

Trained and commissioned Evangelizer at St Mary's Catholic Church, Aiyetoro, Osogbo, Osun State.

Bible animator for 9 years.

Co-ordinator of the Overcomers Prayer Group for 3 years.

Member of the Catholic Charismatic Renewal of Nigeria.

Intercessor and Treasurer of the Prayer Group.

Member of the Parish Pastoral Council.

Secretary of the Catholic Women Organization for St Mary's Catholic Church Aiyetoro.

Instructor on Marriage and Family Life Program.

Lector in the Church.

Merit Awards: Most Responsible Female Graduand, Osun State College of Education, Ilesha, in 1993.

Virtuous Woman, Catholic Women Organization, St Mary's Catholic Church Aiyetoro, Osogbo.

Hobbies: Netball, Hockey, Volleyball, 100m and 200m sprint, and attending spiritual programs.

Onyeachisum John Bosco

Nna'm Onyeachisum John Bosco Konye Nwadike was born on the 6th of February, 1962. Our mother addressed him as Nna'm because she believed that he was a reincarnation of her biological father. Onyeachisum means "Let nobody border me." In the other words, "Live and let live." Our paternal mother named him Ogoamaka, which means "good in-law" because she believed that he was the reincarnation of her father-in-law. Bosco was loved by our paternal grandmother and our mother as a result of the bond of reincarnation. Reincarnation is considered a reward for good behaviour. If children obey their parents or exhibit a good relationship with relatives and neighbours, when they grow up and marry, and if their parents have died, the parents will come back to them. This is to make the child happy for being a good representative of the family. Most parents pamper the child that is a reincarnation of their father or mother. I will go into detail further on. Self-motivation, ability and willingness are the key factors for success. I remember early one morning, Onyeachisum had just finished sweeping our compound and off he went to Orlu Town Main Market to do a carrier job. He stayed till late in the evening and everybody was worried because he had never done that before. Papa and Mama didn't know where to look for him. Everybody was praying for a miracle to happen. At eight o'clock, he came back with a reasonable amount of money. Our parents asked him the kind of question Mary and Joseph asked Jesus when he'd left them and gone to the temple: "Why did you do this to us?" He said, "But I told you that I was going to look for a job at Orlu town. We took loads to a remote village and off-loaded them there. We couldn't finish in time." He then handed over the money he'd earned to our father to keep. Papa was thrilled and admired his ambition, determination and effort. Papa started thinking about linking him up with business people.

One day, his teacher, the headmaster of his school, came to offer him a job with his brother, but our father objected to it. Papa decided to send him to someone he knew – John Ahanato's brother – to work for him. Bosco left home to do his apprenticeship training in Jos Plateau State. He did well and was recommended by his boss, and he started his own business in Jos Plateau State. Being an industrious young man, he worked himself up and bought two shops. He trained two young men to manage his business till the hostility of the militants in the North made him abandon his business and come back home.

Motivation and Goal Setting: Motivation is something that pushes you to do something that is uplifting. It is something that gets you out of your comfort zone. When you lack motivation, you will find it difficult to set a goal. I think our younger brother is an example of a self-motivator. He just made the decision to go out to look for a job, and he woke up one morning and set off to do it. His strong will enabled him to reach his goal in spite of unforeseen circumstances beyond his control. He never fears in the eye of the storm. He acts just as Nelson Mandela described:

> **"The greatest glory in living lies not in never falling, but in rising every time we fall."**
>
> - Nelson Mandela
> https://yourstory.com/2014/07/
> nelson-madndela-greatest-glory

Onyeachisum was married in a Roman Catholic Church in Jos where he based his business. He and his wife had four children there and the fifth at home. He was wounded by the arrows of the militants and had to abandon his property. He still suffers from the wound. Being a determined fellow, he re-established at Aba, Abia State, but because of unrest there and unforeseen circumstances at home that were beyond his control, he closed up and returned home to be with his wife and children. Then our cousin helped him and sold him a minibus on hire purchase, but things didn't go well and he abandoned it. Being a man of optimism and strong will, he met with his brother-in-law, engineer Onyajuwu, my immediate younger sister's husband, who helped him start up again at Orlu main market. Now, he is a home-based businessman.

> *"We face challenges and problems in our personal lives, our families, and our organizations unimagined even one and two decades ago. These challenges are not only of a new order of magnitude, they are altogether different in kind."*
>
> -Stephen R. Covey
> The 7 Habits of Highly Effective People
> Powerful Lessons in Personal Change 2004,
> (Forward page).

> *"Your habits determine your outcomes. Successful people don't just drift to top. Getting there requires focused action, personal discipline, and lots of energy every day to make things happen."*
>
> -Jack Canfield
> *The Success Principles (p. 248)*

Nna'm JohnBosco knows how to cope with hardships. Obstacles never stop him towards progress. He has the spirit of pressing on. Just as William James a philosopher has stated about coping with the inevitable thus:

> *"Acceptance of what has happened is the first step to overcome the consequences of any misfortune." Along the road of life there are shocks and jolts and we have to bend like the willow and absorb them inorder to live longer and enjoy a smoother lifetime. We can turn over a new leaf by reading a Mother Goose rhyme. "For every ailment under the sun. there is a remedy or there is none if there be one, try to find it; if there be none mind it."*

Bosco's life has demonstrated all seven habits! He is a carbon copy of our father. He is also peaceful and gentle of heart. He loves to engage in village activities. He is the leader of our village dancing group (women's section). He was head coach of the village football team. He is one of the church ushers. Bosco, like our parents, frowns at injustice and always speaks the truth.

Achievements and Responsibilities: When things turned sour at Jos, he came home and built a three-storey house for his family. Three of his children secured admission to Imo State University. One of them graduated with French as a major, and the others are studying Education Biology and Electrical Engineering. The remaining two are still in secondary and primary schools, doing their best. More power to your elbow. Progress is part of our family gratification.

Chigoziri Christina Konye Nwadike (nee Konye)

Chigoziri is popularly known as Ahubelem-Ihenmangaodi (special child) because our mother believed that Chigo was the reincarnation of her mother-in-law. She was born in 1964 and is the baby of the family. She is loved by everybody and pampered by everybody. She was baptised like the others in the Catholic Church even though our parents were non-Christian then. After secondary school, she devoted herself to business. She is hardworking, like our parents, and generous and caring. She is a very determined, self-sufficient and thoughtful lady. One cannot deceive her. God bless you, Chigo.

Chapter Three

A Gallery of Functions of the Family

Papa held the "ofor" of the family. This is a wooden or bronze staff signifying leadership and authority. Before he died, he handed over the ofor to his first son Ikechi.

Social Functions: Our mother was a good dancer. She was always the number one in the line in her dancing groups. Dede'm was the leader of his group in the Ebebu dance. I was also the leader of my age grade dancing group in the village.

Educational Activity: The family was one of the pioneers of education. Though our parents were not educated, almost all their children were educated to a high level. We are among the educated classes.

Religious Activities: There are two kinds of religion in Igboland: traditional religion and Christianity. We were adherents of both religions. Our parents were among the traditional religious adherents before they converted to Catholicism, while the rest of us are Christians.

Community Administration: Our family plays a major role in the day-to-day government of the community – cultural activities, political activity and entertainment (dances). Our elder brother used to be the community secretary. John Bosco, our young brother, was our village football coach and in charge of the village women's dance group. He is one of the ushers in our local church.

Chapter Four

The Prestigious Accomplishments of the Family

In this chapter, I am going to exhibit the prestigious achievements of the entire family. My exhibition begins with our parents, who had ten children, one of whom passed on. They were able to raise and educate nine of us. Papa and Mama nurtured us and watched us grow in wisdom, understanding and skills. I am pleased to quote what one of the Black British women said when she attained her desired goal.

> *"Studying has allowed me to be more disciplined in getting closer to my aspirations in life. It has also helped me to develop and enhance skills I already had, but didn't quite know how to utilise. It is my own personal achievement in life that no-one can*

> *ever take away from me because I have earned and worked hard for it.*
>
> *- Beverley Michaels*
> *Pride of Black British Women 1995 (p. 25)*
> *By Deborah King*

Our parents worked hard and went through many ordeals to raise us. Therefore, we are proud to call them our parents, and no one could change their noble title. We, their children, who made ardent efforts to attain our goals, join Beverley Michaels in claiming that no one can ever take away from us that which we have earned and worked for, in life or in death. Our parents and some of our siblings are no more, but their good deeds and achievements cannot be wiped away. They are still remembered.

Stephen R. Covey said:

> *"You can plan for a success by laying out your plan according to the natural law that creates the result - success. One can start by putting up a plan that has uprising steps of execution after compiling talents, strengths, and creativity as needed for the processes with a provision for the unexpected challenges. When one step is well done, that step becomes a habitualized nucleus model imparting self-reliance in moving up the ladder for the next*

rung step. In time, all the steps, with each at a pivotal point of success, display a panorama of good inventory of victories. As progress goes on from one step to another, what has been achieved becomes a motivator for more movement and the rest of the way presents a regular routine of a joyful ride."

- Stephen R. Covey
The 7 Habits of Highly Effective People.
https://succeedfeed.com/stephen-covey

Let us elaborate on the story of the tortoise and the dog. The tortoise challenged the dog to a race. The dog laughed but agreed to compete. The dog was a fast runner and was complacent about the race. The slow-moving tortoise had to plan how-to run-in order to win the trophy. On the appointed day, the tortoise, being a canny animal, cooked dog's food with uraturu – a sleep-inducing herb – and placed it next to the running track. At the scheduled time, the animals set off on the race. The dog ran fast, but on his way, he came upon some food that smelt appetizing. He decided to have a bite since the tortoise was still miles behind. He gobbled up the food and soon felt drowsy, and he fell asleep at the side of the track. The tortoise inched his way one along until he reached the scene of his plan. Exactly as he expected, he saw the dog fast asleep. The tortoise cautiously passed by and proceeded to the finish line. The tortoise, the man with a plan, got the victor's crown of laurel leaves. Life is like this. Those who go out with a plan come back with a crown of victory, but those without a plan never make it. Based on my life experiences, one can make a huge success of life without being intellectual but with a good plan and focus. The family of Konye Nwadike is full of people who followed the plan of their parents. The trend of educational progress is emulated by generation after generation (umukwurumu). The Konyes went from step one to the top rung of the ladder of education and human well-being. Education did not end with Dede'm Ikechi since it has become the tradition of the family; most of us followed suit. As you read along, you will see the progress we made.

In 1980. Dede'm Ikechi Sylvester Konye in his NCE graduation gown. This illustrates the ethos of self-actualization of the Konye family.

Dada'm Agwunihu Cordelia's graduation cap. Dada'm, congratulations on your success.

In 1999. My School President awarding me my Bachelor's Degree in Computer Information Systems. In 2001. The Dean awarding me my Master's Degree in Business Administration. I was on the Honour Roll.

In 2002. Rev. Sr. Chinedum Konye Nwadike, HFSN. Doctor of Philosophy Psychology.

Uloaku Ngozie Livina Konye Nwadike (Mrs. Engineer Declan Onyeajuwu). She finished her teacher training and taught for many years.

Empower yourself and succeed. Come out from your comfort zone, improve your potential and shine. Keep away from the anchors; otherwise, they will drag you down. Maintain your self-confidence. Here is a wonderful insight from a famous self-confidence enhancer:

> *"Hang out with the radiators*
> *As you move on to develop a successful and confident future, the last thing you want is to be surrounded by a bunch of losers whose only pleasure in life is entering the 'victim of the year' competition. Think for a moment about your circle of friends. Do they offer you something? Do they inspire you? Do they enthuse about your dreams? Do they join in the celebrations when you achieve something big? Do they give you as much time as you give them? Think of each friend individually. If the answer is yes, hold on to them. If, on the other hand, it is a definite no, bin them. Stop taking their calls and when they have a tantrum because you haven't been listening to all that's happening in their lives, simply ignore them. This also applies to partners. If all they do is moan, groan and pull you down, bin them. They offer you nothing and are, quite frankly, a drain on your life. You deserve better."*
>
> - Steve Miller
> 7 Secrets of Confidence 2010, (p. 271)

Being around the Marist Brothers, my indigenous reverend sisters, priests and religious changed my life. They motivated me to be what I am today. From each person I encountered, I learnt something unique. For instance, I learnt to love reading books from Brother Ezetulugo of the Marist Brothers of the Schools and also from one of my classmates who loved to read and research different authors. I still love to read, but my engagements often inhibit me from doing so. My nephew, Leonard, always loved to be around me when he was growing up. My style of life influenced him, and he is now a priest. He is happy, I am happy, and everybody is happy with us.

Imitate someone in what would be of benefit to you and others. Allow yourself to be influenced positively, not negatively. Be fruitful so that others will feed on you. It is a blessing if you can make a difference. Be a light to others – a light to your families, a light to your village, a light to your town and a light to the whole world. My parents were light of this kind because their children are all around the world. We have a priest ministering in the Western world, we have a revered sister evangelizing in another part of the word, and we have people in all walks of life serving others.

Chapter Five

Photographs from the Family Album

Parental Blessings and their Effect on Children

In 1970. Papa Konyezuruyahu Mmuoegbulem John Nwadike wearing his Biafra suit, his wristwatch and the only pair of shoes he wore. Papa lived a contented life. Papa, rest in peace.

In 2005. Mama Ojukwu Monica Agim Konye Nwadike in her Christian Mother's uniform, wearin g her necklace cross and a golden wrist ring. Mama, rest in peace.

In 2009. Mama and her grandchildren, as well as our younger brother John Bosco and his wife Anthonia had taken this picture on the 4th of December 2009, a few days before she expired. All of them received special blessings from her. She went to eternity on the 12th of December, 2009, at 4:45pm. Mama, we love you and we are proud of you. Mama Monica was 95 years old when she took this picture. Rest in peace. Within a few days, Mama was no more. That day, her priest ministered to her, she went to confession, received Holy Common and was blessed by the priest. In the morning, when I wanted to give her a shower, Antonia refused. I held Mama and asked her whether she had blessed Antonina, and she answered yes; Antonina confirmed it. Mama, may your blessings always remain with us – Amen.

In 1967. Dede'm Ikechi In 2012. Rest in peace.

In 1992. Dada'm Udaaku Clementina Alisigwe (nee Konye) on her wedding day. She passed on in 2005. Dada'm, rest in peace.

In 1950. Onyemachi Konye. Rest in peace.

In 2013. Dada'm Mrs. Ngamaeme Jeanefrances Dim (nee Konye). Like our mother, she gave birth to ten children. She is a gentle and kind-hearted woman, a patient mother who hates injustice. All of us inherited this virtue of fighting injustice from both our parents. We believe in live and let live, and this is part of our family pride – to God be the glory.

In 2012. Mrs. Anyajiwe Henrietta Odikanwa (nee Konye). She fights injustice single-handedly, like our parents. Dada'm, do not be afraid; God is always on your side. No one can hurt you if you are determined to do only that which is right. If you do have to suffer for being good, you will count it a blessing (1 Peter 3-13).

In 2014. Mrs. Agwunihu Cordelia Nwosu (nee Konye).
A retired educationist (1976-2015) full of wisdom and insight; a happy and fulfilled mother of five children.

In 1980. Rose Ann Nkechinyerem (nee Konye), now Reverend Sister Chinedum Joachim. I began my journey "from here to there" – religious life/USA/UK – and am still on the way to heaven. Surely His goodness and kindness shall follow me all the days of my life (Psalm 23).

In 2001. Mrs Livina Engineer Onyeajukwu (nee Konye). A retired teacher, a businesswoman and a prayer warrior. Livy, keep it up.

In 1967. Nne'm Onyeachisum John Bosco Konye is a business manager and a father of five children. A man of peace and justice. A truth speaker like our parents. A foresighted and hardworking man. More power to your elbow.

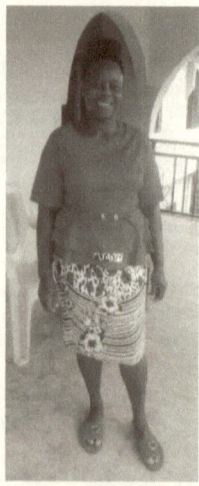

In 2001. Chigoziri Christiana (nee Konye) is a business manager. She is very prayerful, kind-hearted and a fighter of injustice. May the good Lord bless all your endeavours.

In 1970. Mama and papa.

In 2001. I left the USA for Nigeria to visit Mama. Mama was happy to see me as a reverend sister, as she had wished and prayed for. I was also very enthusiastic about her being one of the Christian Mothers. Mama Monica, rest in peace.

In 1995. My Final Commitment at Assumpta Cathedral, Owerri, Imo State. Mama witnessing.

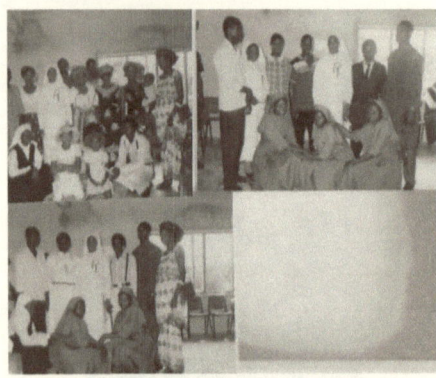

In 1990. First Religious Profession with family and friends.

In 2015. Religious Attainment. Celebrating my Silver Jubilee on the 22nd of August, 2015.

I am a living witness of parental blessings on their children. In 1973, my immediate younger sister, Nne'm Livina, her immediate younger brother, Nna'm John Bosco, and I were standing in front of our old house chatting with our mother, and at one point, she started blessing three of us. She first turned to Bosco and said, "Nna'm Bosco, since you said you have chosen to be a trader, your business will go well for you." Then she turned to Livina and said, "Nne'm" Livy, you will marry a good husband, and you will live in peace with your husband." Then she turned towards me and said, "Nne'm Rosa, Nkechinyerem, you will be a Reverend Sister." I immediately objected, although in pretence, because I didn't want to show that I was interested because I was uncertain. But she reinforced it by saying, "Nne'm, I have said so. **Chineke ga edu gi**." (That is, God will lead you.) And within me, I responded, "Amen and Amen." It happened as she wished it. My name, Chinedum, originated from her wishful thought, so I chose Chinedum (God leads me) during my first profession initiation. Mama, as well as God, called me into this religious life; I believe so because I have met with a lot of obstacles along the way that might have caused me to walk away from this life, but my mother's blessings and those of Almighty God have sustained me on this journey. For instance, whenever she was making supplication to her ancestors, she would call me to stand by her side. She would always want me to watch what she was doing. Each time,

I pondered in my heart why? And why was it always me she called? This order from Mama was the way, according to her, her ancestor had directed her, but I would object to that. Mama's relationship with me made me think that she saw something special in me.

It happened to the three of us as just as Mama had spoken. I was told by one of my elder siblings that the way Mama regarded me was the way she regarded our late brother, Onyemaechi, whom she used to call a prophet. Mama used to call me "Bishop Nwaedo", whom she regarded as a righteous bishop, because there were certain things I never tolerated when I was growing up. Also, whenever my father was making his yearly thanksgiving sacrifice in his shrine, he would love me to stand behind him and listen to what he was saying to his ancestors. After the sacrifice, he would ask me to send the slaughtered hen and cockerel to my mother to prepare for a meal. Then, I usually said no because I did not believe in their Chi, that is, their ancestors. Well, that was my own little understanding then, but now I realise that they were worshipping the true God in their understanding of pure hearts.

Nevertheless, our parents' blessings were effective in our lives. We are happy that Papa and Mama lived to witness the fruitfulness of their blessings on their children and some of their grandchildren. I remember when Papa and Mama gave their blessings to all their grandchildren, both born and unborn. The evidence is in the first three: Chinadozi O. Leonard Dim (now a priest), Kelechi Camillus Odikanwa (now a business manager) and Ijeoma Juliet Nwosu (Mrs. Alagwu) now a nurse. In the next picture, Father Leonard and I portray the blessings of our ancestors.

In 2011 after Deaconate Ordination. "It takes a village to raise a child," and it takes the family of Dim and Konye to raise a priest and a reverend sister in our midst. The fruit of our ancestral legacy. The power of motivation and upliftment.

In 2012. Priestly Ordination.

Family Team Counselling on Positive Thinking and Effective Decision Making

Eight Words that can Transform Your Life

The right choice of positive thoughts will put us on the high road to solving all problems. The Roman emperor, Marcus Aurelius (161-180 AD), once said in eight words: "Our life is what our thoughts make it." If we think happy thoughts, we will be happy. If we think miserable thoughts, we will be miserable. If we think fearful thoughts, we will be fearful. If we think sickly thoughts, we will be ill. If we think failure, we will fail. Always try to have positive thoughts. I use my nephew, Chinedozie, as an example. When he was approached and advised to attend seminary, he accepted it and embraced it with a positive mind. And he maintained positive thoughts about his seminary pursuit till he successfully made it. What one believes works for one. He believed and it worked for him. According to Scripture, discipline is "to discern the sayings of understanding, to receive insight, righteousness, judgment, and uprightness, to give to the inexperienced ones shrewdness (intelligence), to a young man knowledge and thinking ability" (Ephesians 6:11). "Put on the complete suit of armour (truth) from God that you may be able to stand firm against the manoeuvrings of the devil."

Traditional Igbo Naming Ceremony at Birth

The child is a boy. The father has selected a name for him: Chukwuma. The man who will first call the boy Chukwuma will come with a live gift such as a she-goat or a hen that can reproduce and multiply. The father will also produce a cockerel for offering to the ancestors. When it is time, they assemble at the shrine of the family. The father whispers the name to the man who will first use that name. Then the man, with his gift of a she-goat, pronounces, "Chukwuma, I honour you with this gift." Then the father will offer the cockerel, yams, kola nuts, palm wine and oseoji to the gods and ancestors to bless the boy with the name Chukwuma. The kola nuts will be broken, a libation of palm wine will be poured and the blood of the cockerel will be sprinkled around the shrine. The meat of the cockerel will be shared according to the hierarchy of the people present: the host father, the name announcer, the elders, and ohali. The mother of the boy will prepare a meal of yam fufu with delicious soup. The father will offer the fufu meal to the gods, and the mother will feed the boy with the mashed yam (abubo) and the chicken soup. Now the boy is called Chukwuma, meaning God knows.

Grandchildren and Great-Grandchildren

Papa and Mama were blessed to see most of their grandchildren and great-grandchildren. The couple had thirty-five grandchildren and sixteen great-grandchildren:

Children of the late Mr. Ikechi Sylvester Konye

1. Chisom Konye
2. Ms. Mmachi Constance Konye (medical student; Imo State University graduate)
3. Ms. Jacqueline Konye (student)
4. Master Ikechukwu Jerry Konye (student)
5. Master Izuchukwu Franklin Konye (just passed on)

Udaaka Clementina Konye Mrs. Alisigwe

Passed on 2005. No Children

Children of Ngamaeme Jeanefrances Konye (Mrs. Dim).

1. Rev. Father Chinedozi Onyeukwu Leonard Dim (parish priest in the USA)
2. Nkemakolam Desmond Dim (Jos-based business manager)
3. Onyemaucheckwu Ferdinand Dim (graduate Federal University Technology, Owerri (FUTO); Civil-Servant in the USA)
4. Ahamefule Michael Dim (Lagos-based business manager)
5. Chinoso Brendan Dim (Benue State University, Mathematician)
6. Okwuchukwu Remingius Dim (Law graduate, Imo State University)
7. Mr Onyekachi Franklin Dim (business)
8. Odinachiukwu Bibiana Dim (Imo State University)

Children of Anyajiwe Henrietta Konye (Mrs. Odikanwa)

1. Mr. Kelechi Camillus Odikanwa (Lagos-based business manager)
2. Mr. Kasarachi Cornelius Odikanwa (Lagos-based business manager)
3. Mrs. Chinyere Juliet Omezere (registered nurse – Spain)
4. Mr. Chinenye Vitalis Odikanwa (Austria)
5. Ms. Ifeoma Ruphina Francis Umunna (graduate Microbiology, Imo State University)
6. Mr. Ikenna Jeanarous Odikanwa (Thailand)
7. Ms. Oluchi Zita Odikanwa (graduate, Imo State University, Nutrition and Dietetics)

Children of Agwunihu Cordelia Konye (Mrs. Nwosu)

1. Mrs. Ijeoma Juliet Alagwu (registered nurse – USA)
2. Ikechukwu Benedict Nwosu (graduate, Poly Technic, Umuagwo, based overseas)
3. Mrs. Chinaemerem Irene Okoroji (student nurse, Amaigbo Nursing Institution)
4. Eberchukwu Joachim Nwosu (student of Information Technology)
5. Oluchukwu Michael Nwosu (student BSC Orlu)

Reverend Sr. Chinedum Konye Nwadike, HFSN.

Children of Mrs. Uloaku Ngozi Livina Onyeajuwa (nee Konye)

1. Ugochukwu James Adikaibe (BSc. Electrical Engineering).
2. Chinedum Augustine Adikaibe (University Graduate).
3. Chinenyenwa Emmanuel Adikaibe (Mathematician).
4. Chinonso Gabriel Adikaibe (BSc Parasitology and Entomology).
5. Chukwuemeka Michael Adikaibe (BA Education English).

Children of Mr. Onyeachusim JohnBosco Konye

1. Ugochukwu Paschal Konye Graduate (Imo State University, French).
2. Chigozie Vincent Konye (Imo State University, Electrician/Technician).
3. Chinyere Vivian Konye (Imo State University, Education Biology).
4. Chideraa Christopher Konye (Secondary School)
5. Chikwadom Favour Konye (Secondary School)

Chigoziri Christiana Konye

Single, no children

Nephews and Nieces

The Children of Nkemakolam Desmond Dim
3 children

The Children of Onyemaucheckwu Ferdinand Dim
3 children

The Children of Juliet Cynthia Odikanwa Omeozere
3 Children

The Children of Ijeoma Juliet Alagwu
4 children

The Children of Chinemerem Irene Nwosu Okoroji
3 children

God has blessed my parents with thirty-five grandchildren and sixteen great-grandchildren as I am writing this legacy. More great children are coming up from nieces and nephews. Blessed be God who blessed my parents with responsible children. All my siblings are living happily in their married lives except my elder brother, Ikechi Sylvester, who died tragically as a result of his estrangement from his wife. It was most unfortunate. The happiness he enjoyed when he was growing up among us vanished. I am advising you, the young generation, to look well before you marry so that God will bless you as he blessed our parents. An Igbo adage says, *Agwa bu nma*. (Good character is beauty.) Never marry a woman because she is beautiful or a man because he is handsome or has money, but marry him or her as a result of his or her good behaviour. Read Ecclesiasticus 26:1-23. This portrays the right wife to yearn for.

Our First Nephew – Chinedozi Onyeukwu Leonard Dim

Priestly Journey

When our nephew, Chinedozi, was ten years old, he showed early signs of academic brilliance. I encouraged him to take the common entrance examination to join the Marist Brothers or junior seminary. He told me that his dad would not allow him to go to seminary school because he was the first child of the family. My mother, who was with us then, challenged him and said, "Hush, my grandchild, listen to your sister." Then he ran home and came back in the evening to tell our mother that his father had said exactly what he had expected. Our mother and I intervened and encouraged him to proceed, taking no notice of his father. I promised him all my secondary school textbooks if they were the same books he would use. He went ahead, and I tried to assist him as much as I could until he became what he is today.

The reason he made it successfully is that he paid attention to the advice of his elders. When Chi finished his class five in the junior seminary, Umuowa, he wrote to me and told me that he had finished his secondary education. I tried to assess whether he was still interested in priestly ministry; I wrote to him advising him to go into the world to do business for a while. He was mad with me and wrote a lengthy letter expressing his anger. I wrote back to him saying that I would not come between him and his God. I ended the letter in this way: "If you are still eager to proceed, one thing should help you to succeed." Then, I signed my name. When he replied to the letter, he asked, "Dada'm, what is that thing?" I wrote in reply, "Obedience." Then I advised him that whenever he began his training in the seminary, and anytime he went for apostolic work, he should obey his priest and do any kind of work he assigned him to do, except wrong-doing. Don't mind the kind of work. Even if it is washing the dishes or cooking, do it; it will never take anything from you. Moreover, I gave him a mandate that after each apostolic work, he should send me the report letter his priest issued to him. I also told him that he was a handsome young boy, so his priests might test his pride to see whether he was loyal.

Father Chinedozi's parents, Mama Monica, Dede'm Ikechi, Lady Theresa Agu and I, together with all our family members, formed a united team to support his journey to the priesthood. Thank God, he heeded our advice and directives that sustained him. He was ordained as a priest on the 4th of May, 2012. Today, Fr. Chinedozi, Onyeukwu Leonard Dim, is the pride and the legacy of the Konye Nwadike family. It is an enormous blessing that my mother and I introduced him to the court of God. Chi, thanks for being the joy of our family. Our younger generation will follow in your footsteps.

"I gave my fate to God to guide me...
As God had always been gracious to me, he directed
me to the diocese of Palm Beach."

- Leonard Onyeukwu Dim

An Article Published During His Deaconate Ordination: "From Nigeria to Palm Beach" - Leonard Dim's Amazing Journey to Find His New Home - by Linda Reeves of the Florida Catholic Staff, June 17-30, 2011.

Palm Beach Gardens: The excitement builds as a seminarian here comes closer to becoming the first African priest ordained for the Diocese of Palm Beach. Leonard Onyeukwu Dim, 39, will be ordained a transitional deacon June 25. Then he will resume his amazing journey with aims on the priesthood, hoping to be ordained next year. "I admire him because he left behind his country and his family to come to our Diocese to serve the people of God," said Consuelo Minutoli, Office of Vocations Administration Assistant, the first contact Dim made here. "His love for God is so strong that he is willing to come to a strange country alone to serve the people of God," Minutololi added. "He knows in his soul that God has called him to preach in another land. That takes a lot of love for God." All are encouraged to join in celebrations next week at Emmanuel in Boca Raton. Participation will be in keeping with the Diocesan mission to promote vocations and create "a culture of vocations" in the Diocese. "We love him here at Emmanuel," said father Theo Ihedoro, a priest from the Diocese of Owerri in Nigeria, working in the Diocese since 2003 and serving at Emmanuel. "He is very hardworking and ambitious." "We are called the Igbo heartland State," Dim explained. The inhabitants are mostly Igbos, an ethnic group with unique traditions, music, dress and language. "My vocation journey would have been impossible some years ago in Igbo land and culture," he explained. The reason for this was that every first son is regarded as the immediate heir of their family, maintaining the line of culture, and would have been ridiculed and termed a failure to the community for allowing this to happen. Thanks to God that it is not the same today."

Dim is the oldest child born to Jane and Leonard Dim Sr. The family has seven boys and a baby girl. "All the family members are active Catholics," said Dim. His father was a policeman and his mother is a stay-at-home mom. Religion occupies a central place in the lives of most of the residents that live in this part of the world. The people are predominantly

Catholic, and St. Patrick is the patron saint of the region, stemming back to Irish missionaries, who influenced Catholicism there. Dim doesn't recall a time when he did not want to become a priest, but it was his close and nurturing family that provided the "solid background for his entry into the seminary," he said. "My aunt, Chinedum Konye Nwadike, was instrumental to my interest in religious affairs," he said. She is a member of the Holy Family Sisters of the Needy community and enjoyed taking her nephew to church and teaching him about the faith. "I would ask her how priests are made," Dim shared. "She would tell me the bishop would call them, and they would say 'Here I am.'" When he was young, Dim thought that entering the priesthood was simply a matter of being summoned, standing up and walking down the church aisle. He didn't know that his walk would involve four decades and three countries.

At age 10, Dim's prayer life was amazing. He recited the rosary in the morning and led a prayer group every evening with his aunt, Theresa Agu, another great influence. At 13, he requested to enter the seminary in the Diocese of Orlu, living on campus and studying six years. He took several years off for vocations discernment and with clear visions of becoming a priest and serving Nigeria, he entered Seat of Wisdom Seminary, where he earned a bachelor's degree in philosophy in 2000. He served a pastoral year, then traveled to Austria to study German and theology at Karl Franzens University in Graz. Dim shared that he faced enormous challenges leaving his culture, family and language behind, but the cold weather was perhaps the most difficult issue, something he had never experienced. His path took a turn to America when he wanted to brush up on English skills and learn about American culture. He enrolled at Washington Theological Union in Washington, D.C., in January 2007 without a diocesan affiliation and began theology studies.

He had learned that the institute was highly regarded, and that Washington was an interesting city. What he didn't expect was colder weather. Shortly after arriving and during a snowstorm, God put a young man on his path. The student was friendly and from a warm region in the south Dim knew little about – Florida.

> *"I said to myself, 'Wow, I have found a place like my home, Nigeria.' I became so excited to explore Florida. Within a few hours, I was on the Internet."*

As God would have it, Dim's journey through cyberspace to find Florida landed him at www.diocespb.org. He clicked onto the site and found the Diocese of Palm Beach, photos of palm trees and information about the diocesan vocations program. He immediately sent an email.

> *"I gave my fate to God to guide me," Dim said. "As God had always been gracious to me, he directed me to the Diocese of Palm Beach. Within six hours, I received a call that said, 'Hi, Leonard, this is from the Office of Vocations of Diocese of Palm Beach and my name is Consuelo Minutoli.'"*
>
> "I arrived in Palm Beach May 2007," he said.

Accepted into the formation program, Dim began studies at St. Vincent de Paul Regional Seminary in Boynton Beach, served a pastoral year at St. Juliana Parish in West Palm Beach, and has helped out at Emmanuel, the place he calls home. "He has persevered and celebrated his journey towards priesthood with courage and faith," said Father Louis Guerin, formation adviser at St. Vincent de Paul Seminary. "Leonard is a conscientious student and it has been a pleasure to walk with him on this journey."

Our family life and journey are like that of the biblical mustard seed; we began with one man, Konye, then Ojukwu Konye, then we spread to the whole world. We are in our home, Igboland, Biafra in (Nigeria), in the whole of Africa and beyond. God is leading the way and we follow Him. This is our joy, and this is our pride. Dim Onyeukwu found his feet on the soil of Palm Beach as a result of good role modelling and influences. This is the ultimate goal of our family, to lead, to guide, to direct and to uplift. Chinedozi, as our mother, your grandmother (Mamankeukuw gi), named you, thanks for giving our family the highest honour and uplifting the pride of our ancestral lineage; more power to your elbow. Now he is a priest like Melchizedek of old. Chinedozi, the first grandchild of our parents, is also the first child of his parents and the first African priest ordained in Palm Beach, Florida. His priestly journey began with Mama and me. The two of us introduced him and gave him special blessings that led him through. Fr. Chi was fond of his Mamayankeukwu'm, our mother. He is also fond of me, and he still calls me "Dada'm", even as a priest. He has transferred this legacy of mamankeukwu'm and Dada'm to all his siblings. This shows the kind of peace and unity we enjoy in our midst.

In 2012. Rev. Fr. Leonard Onyeukwu Dim celebrating his first Mass in the USA with his fellow Priests and the faithful.

In 2012. Rev. Fr. Chinedozi, the first grandchild of Konye and Monica Konye Nwadike, the pride of our lineage.

In 2013. Rev. Fr. Chinedozi and family members – the fruit and pride of our parents – after his first Mass in our motherland. My sisters, Henrietta and Livina, as well as John Bosco's wife (in red blouse) and various nieces, nephews and cousins formed a team of supporters.

Throughout my writing, I base my narration on the facts. I have told how our mother and I introduced Father Dim to the priestly lineage and supported him with our blessings, prayers and material things. Here is his letter of appreciation to me on the occasion of my Silver Jubilee on the 22nd of August 2015.

Dada-m Rev. Sr. Dr. Chinedum Joachim Konye Nwadike, **HFSN.**

I would like you to know that I appreciate the assistance and favor you have showered on me since I was a child. Jesus said, "Leave the children alone and do not hinder them from coming to me; for the kingdom of the heaven belongs to such as these." Matthew 19:14. I believe  with your teachings and principles; you have indeed made a difference in my life as a child and now a man called to serve God and His people. I remember how you encouraged me and directed me to be what…who I am today – a priest of God the Most High. Jesus said to them, "Truly I tell you, at the renewal of all things, when the Son of Man sits on his glorious throne, you who have followed me will also sit on twelve thrones, judging the twelve tribes of Israel. And everyone who has left houses or brothers or sisters or father or mother or wife or children or fields for my sake will receive a hundred times as much and will inherit eternal life." Matthew

19:28-29. No words can express my gratitude and adoration that I have towards you. The integrity and passion for my good and the good of humanity is worthy of Christ Jesus. Blessed are you who directs all to Truth and service to God! I will forever hold every special memory on my journey of life and smile inside and out when I think of you and all you have done for the Kingdom of God. I hope this collection of words written to you can somehow express my heartfelt gratitude to you, for teaching me what is good to do and what is not. You made me understand how to grow up with others and feel for them even when they may feel they don't belong. You were one of the first to let me know how to share my bread and care for others, and I continue to share my blessings with the people around me to date. I would further say that you are one of my biggest blessings, and forever I want you to know and understand that I am indeed loved and treasured by you. I hope that this letter finds you in the best of your health and I once again thank you for giving me the **greatest of precious gifts, my vocation in the lifelong commitment in the priesthood.** Know that I will forever have you in my prayers in this life and the next. You are blessed who labor in the Lord's vineyard, your reward is great! Respectfully yours in Christ, Father Leonard Dim, called to serve the King of Kings for His Glory!

Thanks, Father, you really proved to me that one good turn deserves another. I am always very grateful to you for making us proud. May the almighty God continue leading you and protecting you from all evil – Amen. As I have told you beforehand, silver and gold I am not expecting from you; rather, be a good ambassador of our families. Always count on my prayers for you. (Chinedozi means "God grooms").

Mr. Kelechi Camillus Odikanwa

Mr. Kelechi Camillus Odikanwa is the second grandchild of our parents. He finished his secondary school and decided to go into business. He is doing well and extending his success towards his siblings by training them in all walks of life. He also extends his generosity to all around him. He is one of the role models of our lineage. Kelechi, may the good Lord continue showing His blessings upon you as you are a leading light to others. (Kelechi means "Gratitude to God").

Mr. Kelechi Camillus Odikanwa

Mrs. Ijeoma Juliet Alagwu (nee Nwosu)

In 2015. Mrs. Ijeoma Juliet Alagwu with her husband and family. She is the third grandchild of our parents and a registered nurse. Her mum is the one carrying a baby on her laps.

Ugochukwu James Adikaibe

In 2018. Ugochukwu is the fourth grandchild of our parents. Ugo is a role model to his family. He is a university graduate, and his siblings are following in his footsteps. He works hard just like our parents. May the good Lord always be with you and all our generation who are striving towards success and living good lives as our parents taught us. (Ugochukwu means "Crown of God").

Ugochukwu Paschal Konye

In 2018. Ugo is the fifth grandchild of our parents. He is striving hard to live according to the norms of our parents. May the Almighty God be a leading light to your ways. He is a graduate of Imo State University. He earned his degree in French. During his one-year study experience in Benin, a French-speaking country, he became fluent in French. When he was about to go to Benin, he was placed in the first group but had no money, so he did not go. He was assigned to the second group but did not make it as a result of financial constraints. He kept on striving to raise funds till he succeeded and then joined the last group. When he arrived, he worked very hard. He told me that he remembered his grandmother's proverb that the poor man's child is "always wise." He also said to me, "Auntie, your wise philosophical saying about the mystery of possibilities has helped me a lot. These two adages led me through and really kept me focused." Then, at his leisure, he started learning to make some bags like these below.

Ugo's products made in Benin 2018.

When I received all these well-designed bags in my WhatsApp chat, I said, "Who is this person that thinks I am a businesswoman?" I checked it carefully and it was Ugo! I called him immediately to caution him against wasting his time searching for all these beautiful bags. He said to me, "Ma, I made them myself." He sent me a video of himself seated on the floor producing them. I was overwhelmed and thrilled. I was uplifted and cherished him. This is what I have been talking about – the pride of my family and the legacy of our parents. What amazed me is that he said to me, "Ma, you taught me that. In your book *The Pride of My Family*, you quoted Martin Luther King Jr. saying, 'knowing to run, walk or crawl. If you can't fly, then run, if you can't run, then walk, if you can't walk, then crawl, but whatever you do, you have to keep moving forward.' This is my aspiration and guide. For this reason, I want to follow your footprints and those of our grandparents. Thanks, so much Ma for your wonderful thought of writing that book. I am proud of you being part of my lineage." Ugo went on and whispered to me, "Based on my experiences I chose to write this article 'Better Late Than Never' when our lecturer asked us to select a topic to write on." One can see here the impact of motivation and role modelling on young people. Believe it or not, children always copy whatever adults do. Therefore, I urge every adult to be mindful of what you say or do in the presence of youngsters because they copy you.

Ugo, more power to your elbow. I advise all students to imitate anyone that could enhance their lives. I would like to cite here the advice of Mother Teresa of Calcutta to all students.

"To students: I pray that all those young people who have graduated, do not carry just a piece of paper with them but that they carry with them love, peace and joy. That they become the sunshine of God's love to our people, the hope of eternal happiness and the burning flame of love wherever they go. That they become carriers of God's love. That they

BETTER LATE THAN NEVER

THE HISTORICAL BACKGROUND:

The proverb was first recorded in 1200. It appeared in several collections of English proverbs. The first time the phrase appears in print in English was in "The Yeoman's Tale from The Canterbury Tales" by Geoffrey Chaucer published in 1386. "For better than never is late; never to succeed would be too long a period."

Better Late Than Never – Essay

DEFINITIONS:

"Better late than never" is an ancient proverb with a deep hidden meaning. Time and again all of us are told to complete the tasks assigned to us on time and being lazy most of us fail to do any assigned work on time. The result is we completely avoid the work and stop doing it further.

Yes it is essential to finish a work on time but what is more important is finishing the work. Here comes the significance of the proverb "better late than never" which means that it is all right to be late in completing an activity than never doing it. What is essential is doing the work.

Better late than never

What's the meaning of the phrase 'Better late than never'?

To arrive or do something later than expected isn't good, but it is better than not at all.

EXPLANATION PROPER:

This proverb can be best explained with the example of the story of the rabbit and the tortoise. Once upon a time, a rabbit and a tortoise decided to compete for a race. The rabbit laughed at the tortoise for even thinking about competing with him and therefore he was confident that he will win. They started the race and the rabbit started running. After a few miles, he turned back and saw that the tortoise was completely out of sight. He thought that the tortoise can never win the race and since it was out of his sight, he decided to take a nap. While he was sleeping the tortoise surpassed him and won the race. Because of the ability of running fast, the rabbit was obviously going to win. But the tortoise very well knew the importance of the phrase "better late than never" and thus it started competing slowly, but steadily and thus won the race. It is also important to note that if an individual starts doing a work, today or tomorrow he or she is bound to finish the work and succeed.

Thinking that it is impossible to complete a work will result in the work being never completed because it was not even started at the first place. It is human nature that when one notices that a work is difficult he or she simply decides to quit, what is important here is to understand the fact that quitting should never even be considered as an option.

Slow and steady can also win the race. All the students are of different nature, if a student decides that he or she will study throughout the year, that individual will stand first or second in the class. There are also students who study a night before the exam. These students also get promoted to the next class. But can a student who does not study at all or who studies after the exam is promoted to the next class. The answer is No: it is better to study late, at the last moment also than to escape studying totally.

ADVERTISEMENTS:

Similarly goes the saying; it is better to complete a task late than never doing it or than avoiding it completely.

By, **Konye paschal ugochukwu**

be able to give what they have received. For they have received not to keep but to share."

- Mother Teresa of Calcutta
The Joy in Loving
Daily Wisdom with Mother Teresa 1996 (p. 46)

In 2013. Grandson and granddaughter of our parents, graduates of Imo State University.

We are many, and I cannot write on individuals one by one, so I write on the first nephews and nieces of each of our families that are grownups. God has blessed us, so we should be grateful to Him. One of the sources of pride of our family is the fact that all my siblings married within our town. We maintain the root of our lineage. Some of my sisters married at Umuna, the birth home of our mother, some married at Umuowa, the birth home of our grandmother, that is, our mother's maternal home, and some married in our own hometown, Orlu. We don't need transportation to visit our sisters and their families. One of the traditions in Igboland is that if a female child lives a wayward life, she must be married outside her clan. So, we are pleased and blessed that that is not our case. We fall into legal citizenship of our clan. It is not our doing but God's.

The Pride of my Family: Mr. Dim Leonard Senior married my sister, Jeanefrances, and they had ten children, just like our parents. Their first child, my first nephew, Leonard Junior, became a reverend father. It is a great privilege to have him in our family.

The witnesses of Father Leo's priestly ordination in the USA on 4th May 2012. With me are the late Mr. Leonard Sr. and Mrs. Jeanefrances Dim (parents of Fr. Leonard Dim Jr., my nephew) and my cousin, Chinedu Agu, a US Soldier. His mother is a younger sister to my mother.

In 2012. Rev. Fr. Hamann is a mentor to our nephew, Fr. Leonard, and the person who made it possible for him to be a priest in the USA. Father Hamann, thanks a lot!

Austrian Flag

Fr. Hamann is an Austrian priest who played a significant role in my nephew's life. Staying with Fr. Hamann in Austria enabled my nephew to learn German, which he now speaks fluently. That is another source of pride in our family. Fr. Hamann is now "Bishop Hamann." This is another extension of blessing. The grace of the Almighty God is still moving in our midst; to Him be the glory.

I agree with Hillary Clinton that "It takes a village to raise a child," but I would go further and say, "It takes the whole world to raise a child."

In 2012. Father Leonard Chinadozi O. Dim and his parents during his priestly ordination. Unfortunately, his father passed on the 20th of July 2015. May he rest in peace.

In 2012. With my cousin, Chinedu Agu, from my maternal lineage. He is a US soldier. This picture was taken during Father Chinedozi's priestly ordination. Behind us is Rev. Sr. Beatrice, my Father Founder's half-sister. We have a whole lot to be proud of. To God Be the glory.

In 2006. In front of the Basilica of the National Shrine of the Immaculate Conception in Washington, DC.

In 2013. In London.

Chapter Six

My Father's Brothers and Sisters

Late Uncle Anuole Basil and Family: As I mentioned earlier, Papa Konye had half-brothers and sisters. His half-brothers were the late Dee Raphael and the late Dee Geoffrey. All these half-brothers and sisters married and had many children. Anytime we have a home-coming, one can see that Amuba's children are a whole nation. The name Amuba means "increase in number." As this name decodes, our family increases to infinity non-stop!

Late Uncle Anuole Basil Nwadike: Nna'm Basil was the immediate junior brother to our father, Konye. He first married Fabiana from Umuowa, and she gave birth to two boys, Chukwuemeka Simon and Ujunwa Lawrence. Unfortunately, she died, and Uncle Anuole then married Julia from Umuna, who gave birth to six children, Chika, Chinyere, Onyebuchi, Azuka, Chukwuma and Ada Oluchi.

Chukwuemeka Simon married Chinyere and has five children.
Ujunwa Lawrence married Chizoba and has three children.

Chika is not yet married.

Chinyere married Oby and has four children
Onyebuchi married Chioma and has one child with more on the way.
Ada Oluchi is yet to marry.

These children of Nna'm Basil are very progressive and married the wives of their choice. The family of Mama Ogoma just keeps on growing. This is also a source of pride in our family. All these eight children are doing well in their various walks of life. Some have graduated from university, while some have finished secondary school and are engaged in business. Some are overseas. The name of our ancestor, Amuba, is really on active service.

Chapter Seven

A Guiding Light to Future Generations

An Igbo adage says, "Power never goes up; rather, it comes down." It is now I come to really understand this proverb. Since my youth, I have enjoyed good health, but now I am paying deposits to mother earth. Years ago, I lost two teeth, and I now wear glasses. I can't read things far away, everything looks cloudy without glasses, and I often struggle to read even with glasses. Whenever we lose some part of our bodies, we are dying. Even shaving your hair is making a bit-by-bit payment to mother earth. We keep on shrinking every day till we shrink no more; that is how nature made it. That is all the more reason why we should endeavour to do as much good as we can. We pass through this precious life only once. Job reminds us that the Lord gave and the Lord has taken… (Job 1:21). So, as long as you live, try to be the pride of those around you by doing some good deeds. Everything we own belongs to God. Be happy, love one another and cherish one another.

In 2014. After successful total thyroidectomy surgery.

Summary

Ninety-nine percent of all failures come from people who have a habit of making excuses.
> \- George Washington Carver
> Chemist who discovered over 325
> uses for the peanut.

Challenges, circumstances, ordeals never stopped our parents in their team effort to raise us and make us the wealthy lineage of Amuba. Their ultimate goal was to make us admirable human beings. Their ambition was to raise us in a manner worthy of emulation: God-fearing, with wisdom and insight, and academically and physically fit. Their wishes were fulfilled with our enormous efforts. We ought to carry on this noble legacy. You need to keep this light of our ancestors and our parents burning. "Never lose sight of your dreams and goals. But make sure you are equipped to carry them through." Avoid **fans** of toxic friends, otherwise they will ruin your career. Jack Canfield called them "toxic people." According to Canfield:

> *"Avoid Toxic People until you reach the point in your self-development where you no longer allow people to affect you with their negativity, you need to avoid toxic people at all costs. You're better off spending time alone than spending time with people who will hold you back with their victim mentality and their mediocre standards. Make a conscious effort to surround yourself with positive, nourishing, and uplifting people – people who believe in you, encourage you to go after your dreams, and applaud your victories. Surround yourself with possibility thinkers, idealists, and visionaries."*

"Surround yourself with successful people."
- Jack Canfield
The Success Principle 2005 (p. 193)

"Things which matter most
Must never be at the mercy of things which matter least."

-Goethe

*"There can be no friendship without confidence,
And no confidence without integrity."*
-Samuel Johnson

Be on your guard,
make good chooses and bin unnecessary ones
-Chinedum Konye Nwadike

Our parents went through many ordeals before they became successful. They never, ever blamed anybody or gave excuses for any problem. In times of difficulty, they reasoned together to resolve their problems and moved on. They refused absolutely to listen to toxic individuals who would have held them back. Therefore, I urge you to be men and women of self-control and integrity. Know what you want and stir up your ability to get it done. Be truthful as Papa and Mama were, no matter the consequences for you. There is a blessing for speaking the truth rather than remaining silent, and another person may be punished because of your silence. Rescue those in danger and God will be your fighter and protector. Man can only punish the flesh but will never touch the soul. Do not be afraid to stand up for justice as our parents did, even though they became victims of injustices. The late Dede'm Ikechi, in his contribution to one of my books, *Building Up Self-confidence A Fundamental Way of Conquering Fear*, said,

"Fear is a feeling caused by the nearness or possibility of danger or evil... This is equally fright, apprehension, and uneasy feeling. Fear can equally be defined as heat inflammation, anxiety, ignorance, error, desire, and caution; all of these are states of being afraid. This is a situation where one becomes apprehensive of the unknown. Example, sickness may cause death, blindness, deafness, dumbness, certain bodily losses, and deformities. To cure fear, remove the error governing fear by telling yourself that there is nothing like fear. Remove fear from your mind. For instance, if you are walking at night, do not think about a snake biting you or think about meeting a ghost on the way. The moment any of these comes into your mind, all other evil thoughts will come into you. At this point, you will start seeing phantoms, hiding animals, and spirits all around you. Next, you start shivering and become sick. Always say to yourself nothing will happen."

- Ikechi S.I. Konye (VC10)
10th December 2010

I believe what he said because whatever you feel and think happens to you. If I can do it and succeed, then you can too. Do not be afraid; rather, keep striving, be focused, be consistent in action. Maintain our family tradition and identity; it is a worthy one and something one should be proud of. Hold onto whatever talent God allots to you. Make use of it to enhance your lives and the lives of others, as our parents did. They were not elites, yet they were able to work hard and give expert advice to us and others. Never bury your talent; rather, dwell in constant improvement to shine. It is not only in academics that one shines, however. Be proud of being businessmen and women. What you need to do is to develop and enhance the skills you already have. That is your own personal achievement that no one can take away from you. Begin from somewhere and, moment by moment, rise to the top. Nobody can do it except you. And no one is born insignificant; you are created for a purpose, period.

> *"Life is like a combination lock; your job is to find the right numbers, in the right order, so you can have anything you want."*
>
> *- Brian Tracy*
> *https://bulewestproperties.com/*
> *life-islife-a-combintion-lock-your...*

God is our shepherd; His goodness and kindness will follow us all the days of our lives. The blessing of our ancestors is still with you. Live exemplary lives. I pray that, as God has called me and Chinedozi to religious and priestly lives, He will continue the call among you. Love one another and help one another in times of difficulty. Carry each other along. May the peace and blessings of God be with you forever – Amen.

The power of belief is the key to self-enhancement, self-empowerment, self-affirmation, and they are the sources of self-actualization. If you intend to achieve self-confidence and conquer fear, first of all, you have to believe in yourself and embark on your journey with a determined effort and willingness to obtain your dream goal. Believing without action yields no effective result. So, be a person of action and always affirm yourself by saying, "I can do it, and I am doing it right now." Try to build strong trust in yourself and always answer, "Here I am Lord; send me" (Isaiah 6:8-9). And add to it, "I am willing and ready to move on and I am equal to the task." You have to be up and doing to gain self-confidence. Self-confidence is the way you shape your life, which is transforming your old primitive self to a new self that gives you an authentic new self-image. Achieving self-confidence and conquering fear means *"read, read, and read"*. What you think of yourself is what you will be.

"As a man thinketh in his heart, so is he…" (Proverbs 23:7). If you rate yourself lazy, ugly, good for nothing, etcetera, that is what you will be; anytime you intend to take up a responsibility, your mind will automatically trigger and remind you, "You cannot do it; you're good for nothing."

In this manner, begin now to sow a seed of self-confidence to reap a healthy harvest. How do you sow the seed? Reinforce yourself with a positive attitude by saying to yourself, "I am able, I can do it, and I am achieving it already." Once you begin to program yourself and know yourself, you start to feel more convinced, confident, and powerful about yourself and your environment. Picture yourself beautiful, smart, happy, gentle, loving, calm and successful. Marian Harrison, a British high-class fashion designer who is proud of her skills said:

> *"I enjoy the freedom and self-satisfaction that comes from being your own boss."*
> - Marian Harrison
> Pride of Black British Women 1995 (p. 42)
> By Deborah King

I agree with Marian Harrison because once you are responsible and skillful, you will feel joyous and fulfilled. Many individuals do not feel fulfilled unless they are medical doctors or presidents or bosses of their organizations. No, that is not true. Even if you are a carpenter, a driver, a gardener, etc. and skillful with it and make your living out of it while helping others, you are a master and captain of your being. Everybody must be something, and what matters is that, whatever you are, cherish and develop it well. Marian Harrison, a fashion designer, is proud of her skill. Are you proud of your skill? If not, why not? Be proud and have the conviction to develop what you already have. This conviction will enable you to build your confidence in yourself, which then helps you to alter anything that inhibits you from functioning effectively. Be self-assured and always maintain a positive frame of mind. Begin now to remove fear and negative thoughts from your vocabulary. Remember, fear is always out there and is already doing those things you are afraid of, but you have to do them anyway.

> *"Make sure you have the career that you want; it is your right. Do not choose a career because another person is doing it. Do it because you're capable to do it and it is what you are inspired to do."*
>
> *- Deborah King*
> *Pride of Black British Women 1995*

Here is a quote to support this:

> *"Everyone has a God-given talent. Discover yours and use it! No 'ifs,' 'ands' or 'buts.' Just do it PERIOD! There is no one without a talent. The question is, do you know how to decipher what that is for yourself, or are you going with the flow?"*
>
> - Margaret Dureke
> Word and Phrases of Wisdom
> For Spiritual and Emotional Upliftment 2002 (p. 10)

Cut your coat according to your cloth (size). Everybody is a unique individual and has unique gifts and talents. Accept your own, develop them, use them and be satisfied. Our parents said to us, "A fly that has no adviser goes to the grave with the corpse."

They asked us to always heed the advice of honourable elders, respect them and "honour your parents and your elders so that you may have long life and may prosper..." (Deuteronomy 5:16). You are advised to listen to the good advice of the elders for your days to be brightened. On the 21st of January 2015, when President Obama was giving his State of the Union Address, he said,

> *"Share your broad vision to each other."*
> - Barack Obama
> 44th U.S. President

I say to you, my people, share your vision with each other, enlighten each other, direct each other, rejoice with each other and bear with one another.

Conclusion

The story goes like this: Three women in a boastful escapade were making claims about which one of them had the most highly prized jewelry. The challenge came to a heated agreement that a day be appointed for them to bring along their precious jewels for a panel of judges to decide who was the richest in jewelry. A day was chosen and judges selected. A fourth woman applied to be included in the competition. She was accepted. On the fixed day, at the agreed venue, contenders displayed their wealth of jewelry. The fourth woman came with her four sons and two daughters, well dressed, simply beautified and well fed. When the judges went around awarding points to the competitors, they came to the woman who exhibited her six children as her six jewels. The judges were astounded at this marvel of expression. They went in to reach a decision. They emerged with a declaration that the woman with six children was the winner of the contest for children were of inestimable worth. And so, in Igboland, this story is epitomized in these names given to children: Omumukaku, Nwakaego, Nwaburu and Nwakaejiekwu.

Ohu nwa bu ohu aku, which means children are greater than wealth. In the same light, Papa Konyezuruyahu Mmuoegbulem Nwadike and Mama Ojukwu Monica Agim Okafor Nwaugbala Konye Nwadike devoted their time to propagating children and established a number of local industries in order to procure the finances needed to educate them. This is a life-long occupation and demands immense determination. What was the result? The children seemingly emulated their parents and made sure that the efforts lavished on them produced the expected goals.

We sing in Igboland: *Digi kpata aku, iwere omumu mezie ya, ihe uwa adakota.* In a short space of time, the Konyes have grown from one man and one woman to sixty people, each with an admirable education and consequently an enviable livelihood. What a blessing!

Every praise and blessing belongs to our God, the God of the Amuba family. He has blessed us and crowned us with his immense goodness and chose us in a special way to increase and multiply. Free us from the oppression of our enemies and grant us the knowledge of freedom. Show your faithful love to all our ancestors. Glory and honour to you, Almighty God, forever and ever – Amen.

Enjoy this book to the full. Good luck!

About the Author

Sr. Chinedum's Graduation Ceremonies.

Rose Ann Nkechinyere Konye Nwadike is a daughter of Ndiowerri Village, Orlu, in Orlu Local Government Area of Imo State in Igboland, Eastern Nigeria. Although she was raised in a non-Christian family, her parents allowed her to become a Catholic. Rose Ann, as she was named in baptism, joined the League Girls, an order of young Catholic girls dedicated to following in the footsteps of the Virgin Mary, Mother of Jesus. Another group she joined was the Confraternity of the Christian Doctrine (CCD), which enabled her to teach Catechism to both children and adults who were preparing for confirmation and holy communion. Among them was her nephew, Reverend Father Leonard Dim. She was also an active member of the St. Anthony of Padua Society. It was through her service with the society that she obtained the inspiration to serve the poor and the needy.

She joined The Holy Family Sisters of the Needy at Nekede, Owerri, and at her first religious commitment took the name Chinedum Joachim, (Chinedum), which means **God leads me**. In 1991, Sr. Chinedum was sent to the United States of America for mission and study. She attained an Associate Degree in Medical Secretarial, with honours, at Lackawanna College, Pennsylvania. She also holds a Bachelor of Science in Computer Information Systems from Strayer University, Washington, DC.

In 1995, Sister Chinedum returned to Nigeria and made her final religious commitment. She then went back to study in the USA and obtained a Master of Science Degree in Business Administration, with honours, at Strayer University, Washington, DC. At Lacrosse University, she earned her PhD in Psychology, summa cum laude. She also gained State of Maryland Board of Nursing Assistant Certification and District of Columbia Nursing Assistant Certification from the University of the District of Columbia, Washington, DC. with a speciality in working with elderly people at the Providence Hospital, Washington DC branch of Carroll Manor. She also worked at the Institute of Psychotherapy with children with challenging behaviours. In the Catholic Archdiocese of Washington, DC, she became involved with the Igbo Catholic community as their chaplain and played a leading role in numerous associations.

Sister Chinedum worked her way through the strict immigration process and became a citizen of the United States of America. Being an American citizen did not deter her from moving to the United Kingdom when she was asked to be a missionary there by the Superior General of her congregation. While in Britain, Sister Chinedum passed the test for Life in the UK and secured her permanent residence permit. Staying in the UK was a lot of fun for her as she worked tirelessly with the Good Counsel Network Apostolate in taking care of vulnerable single mothers, becoming their Assistant House Manager. This led her to enrol in a Module 4 Counselling Skills Course at Cambridge Open College to enable her to help young mothers in pregnancy crises. She was a member of the Association of Christian Counselling and went to the "abortuary centre" (abortion clinics) weekly to counsel pregnant ladies who intended to go for an abortion. Through this mission, she has saved many babies from being aborted.

She extended her spiritual activities to St. Pius X Catholic Church, St. Mary Magdalene Willesden Green in London. Sister Chinedum worked at Windsor Primary School, Play With Us section East Ham, as Childcare Practitioner. She became the first Zonal Superior of The Holy Family Sisters of the Needy English Zone and the first Chair of the HFSN Board of Trustees, UK.

According to Sister Chinedum, our grandmother used to say to her, "Nne-m Nkechinyerem, *oga adiri gi mma* (it shall be well with you)." She told me that she always claimed this word from our grandmother and really, it was well with her. Those who grew up with her are still wondering how she managed to make such a success of her life. Having succeeded in life as a result of our grandmother's counsel, she decided to write this book, *The Pride of My Family*, which will be of benefit to all who read it, especially our younger generation. Sister made a great impact on many peoples' lives, including mine. She is the brain behind what I am today. She motivated me to attain the priesthood ministry. My aunt is someone who lifts and inspires others. Dada'm, I am proud of you. Keep up your good work. I am pleased to contribute to your autobiography.

Rev. Fr. Leonard O. Chinedozi Dim
(Nephew)

Bibliography

Canfield, J. (2005) The Success Principles. New York: Harper Collins Publishers.

Covey, S. R. (2004) The 7 Habits of Highly Effective People. New York: Free Press London Toronto Sydney.

Dureke, M. (2002) Words and Phrases of Wisdom for Spiritual and Emotional Upliftment. Hyattsville Maryland: JAHS Publishing Group.

Erikson, E. (1968) Identity, Youth and Crisis. New York: Norton.

Field, R. (1983) Steps to Freedom: Discourse on the alchemy of the heart. Putney: VT Threshold Books.

Https/www.google.co.uk/search.

https://en.wikipedia.org/wiki/marcus_Aurelius

https://www.quotespedia.org/authors/m/marcus-aurelius/our-life-is-what

Jaya, C. and Edward Le Joly. (1997) The Joy in Loving: A Guide to Daily Wisdom. Great Britain: Penguin Books.

Jerusalem Bible, Popular Edition. (1974) Darton, Longman & Todd.

King, D. (1995) Pride of Black British Women. London: Hansib Publishing Limited.

King, Martin L. Jr. (1960) Breakingmuscle.com/...keep-moving-for...Mobile-friendly,

Living Bible, Catholic edition. (1983) Wheaton, Illinois: Tyndale House.

Nwachukwu, J. H. (2012) From There To Here: A Journey of Hopes and Dreams. Library of Congress Control Number: 2012946095.